In the *Shadow* of the

Stories from Days Long Past

In the *Shadow* of the
ROAN

Stories from Days Long Past

Allen Cook

Chestnut Ridge Publishing

(Second Edition)

In the *Shadow* of the

ROAN

Stories from Days Long Past

Written By: Allen Cook

Researched By: Janie Ledford Cook

Graphic Design: Danielle Garland Cook

Cover Design and Marketing: Danielle Garland Cook

Cover Photograph: Courtesy Library of Congress

Email: *wildestcounty@gmail.com*

Facebook: *www.facebook.com/wildestcountync*

Second Edition 2021

ISBN: 978-0-9908657-2-8

Chestnut Ridge Publishing,
North Carolina

JOHN 3:16 <><

Dedication

This book is dedicated to all the old timers who would sit on their porch or in their favorite chair at the local country store and talk about the old days. Grandpa Charlie Ledford, Great Grandpa Aught Burleson and many other old timers have passed but I hope to keep their stories alive. Thanks for telling a young'un "Stories from Days Long Past." Special thanks to my mother, Janie Ledford Cook, for doing much of the research behind this book and to my wife Danielle Garland Cook for the editing, graphic design and publishing.

-Allen

Contents

Preface

Years of researching old court records, newspaper articles, and recording oral histories from old timers has led to the compilation of the stories in this book. As one reads the book, they will notice that the book is comprised of entertaining stories, documented research and personal commentary. In the stories, I took creative liberty with the characters and crafted the old tales in a way that I thought they might have transpired. The research presented in this book discusses and documents details about the events. Since some of the happenings described have been lost or exaggerated over the years, I feel that this particular format will lead to an accurate recollection of the old timer's oral treasures. Even with thorough documentation and research, many details in this book are open to speculation. As a result, I make no claim that the accounts are entirely true.

In the Shadow of the Roan is very close to my heart. Most of the content involves my direct ancestors. Since this is the second edition of the 1997 book that was originally put together as a family history for my relatives and close friends; it was my desire to keep *In the Shadow of the Roan: Stories from Days Long Past* true to its original form, but also keep it historically accurate. As a result, I took the liberty to clarify and add new details and images to the original stories. I hope you enjoy this expanded and updated edition of an old family favorite.

-Allen

Introduction

Yellow beechnuts and chestnut oaks spread dying leaves over frost bitten ground to pull the covers over the once lush summer flora. But the crimson maples defiantly hold their leaves, crying out to be noticed amongst the gray rocks and deep green firs in the browning woods of Roan Mountain. If there is one feature that stands out in the forest of local history, it is the blood that was shed during the lawless times in the region surrounding Roan Mountain.

The accounts that have been compiled are like the crimson maples on the autumn hillside. Blood stains from an era long forgotten demand to be seen as one researches the annals of mountain history. The rural Appalachian hollows and ridges of the early 1900s were the site of many shootings, lynchings, and knifings. Like the lawless boom towns that sprung up in the old west, many mountaineers would take justice into their own hands and settle disputes with their gun or the hangman's noose. This book will retell stories from days long past and look at some of the injustices that show up as the crimson maples in the shadow of Roan Mountain.

Chapter 1:

First Trip to the Land of Clouds

"Off to the north of the sunset was the Roan, as it had stood for centuries, grim and silent and eternal."

-*The Farmer and Mechanic,* **North Carolina (1909)**

He first heard about the roan colored mountain from a soldier in his Lightening Brigade. Tales of endless mountain top meadows carpeted with lush cool season grasses, towering granite bluffs that touched the clouds and vast native rhododendron gardens planted by the hand of God intrigued the former Union General. Visiting the area on business to tour the Cranberry Iron Ore Mine, General John Wilder was persuaded to take his first trip to the land of the clouds. It would not be his last.

It was a bright and clear late summer morning in Northeast Tennessee. Saddling up at the valley town named Roan Mountain, John Wilder and two local guides set out for Roan Ridge. The metallic click of horse shoes on the hard-packed creek stone road signified the start of the trip. The men conversed about the mineral and iron ore deposits of the region as their horses trotted alongside a gently flowing creek near a settlement called Burbank. Past Burbank, the way got steep and winding as the excursion party gained elevation. Stopping near a springhead, the horses were given a momentary break. During the pause, the younger of the two guides, named Cal, recounted a tale about an unfortunate bear hunter who had become disoriented in the mountain fog and had fallen to his death. As he described the story, the old guide pointed to a nearby outcrop of rocks as the location of the accident.

The older guide in the group went by his last name of Shell. After hearing Cal's story, Shell pointed to a distant mountain. He beat his tobacco pipe out while weaving a tragic tale. The story was about how a deputy from the town of Elizabethton, Tennessee came to "that ridge over yonder" to look for an illegal moonshine distillery. The deputy never returned and was later found by a boy who was squirrel hunting. He had been killed by a single shot to the head. The shooter was still on the loose and the local guides speculated as to who the suspect might be. John Wilder silently pondered the story. The horses were ready to go.

Large tracts of virgin timber bordered the ragged trail up the mountain. Massive chestnuts, red spruce and cherry trees dominated the mountainside. Timbering the steep hills was not economically feasible, the guides explained. While his horse navigated the ancient game trail to the top, Wilder's engineering mind tried to process the logistics of a mountain logging operation.

As the trail got higher, the old-growth deciduous forest transitioned into a mix of beech trees and evergreens. The air was also noticeably cooler. Moss covered rocks and numerous spring heads dotted the damp surroundings. To Wilder, the alpine woods looked like a scene from his childhood home in the Catskills of New York.

It was noon when the party reached Roan Ridge at a pass known as Carver's Gap. At the gap, the dense fir thicket abruptly ended and gave way to a vast and lush ridgetop meadow framed by distant mountain views. The horses were given a well-deserved rest and seemed to enjoy the natural pasture. While the horses grazed, the guides explained the mystery of the high elevation fields, known as balds. The old timer guide said that the Catawba and Cherokee

Photograph of Colonel John Wilder taken during the Civil War. Photo Courtesy Library of Congress. (1861)

Indians would often battle on the balds because it was prime hunting ground and disputed border territory. The legend was that trees were cursed from growing on the blood-soaked ridges due to the many conflicts. The younger guide, Cal, heard a more logical story about how the Indians used to set the balds on fire each winter and how it was too cold and windy for new trees to take root. Wonder filled Wilder's eyes as he heard the local legends.

In the *Shadow* of the
ROAN

In the lush summer grass, a herd of sheep grazed on a distant bald known as Grassy Ridge. Locals from North Carolina and Tennessee used the balds in the summertime to graze livestock. Often old timers would camp with their sheep throughout the summer. There was no shortage of entertaining and interesting tales. Shell stretched out his arms as he told a story of how eagles with massive wing spans snatched lambs from the balds during the spring lambing season. Wilder said that he heard from a soldier in his company that the last elk shot in North Carolina was killed on the Roan just prior to the war. A cool summer breeze drifted over the high elevation expanse as the men swapped stories and admired the vast fields and distant views.

While the guides rounded up the horses, Wilder surveyed the mountains of North Carolina. In the middle of Carver's Gap was the state line and mineral rich Mitchell County. After his trip to the largest iron ore mine in the country at Cranberry Mine in Elk Park, Mitchell County; the famous Union general wondered how many other rich veins of iron ore were waiting to be discovered in the valleys below.

With the horses caught and mounted, the men turned their reins in the direction of a trail leading up the ridge. Their destination was a small level bald just past the highest point of the mountain known as Roan High Knob. After another hour of riding through towering old growth fir trees, the party arrived at their camp site.

The men pitched camp on a level grassy knob surrounded by big sky and facing scenic southern and eastern views of faraway ridges. With the tents set up, the local guides shifted their attention towards tending to the horses and building a fire to fix a backwoods supper. With a few free hours at his disposal, Wilder took off alone to look for the place that Shell called Lion's Bluff. Of course, Wilder got to hear the story about the mountain lion that attacked a teenage boy near that bluff in 1842.

The air was clean and crisp as John Wilder started down the trail away from camp. Following an age old path through a mossy fir forest to its end, Wilder eased his way out of the pines and onto a massive weathered rock formation. A cool western breeze tickled his beard and chilled his sweaty face. The only sound to be heard was the subtle whispers of the wind blowing through the nearby pines. The former Union soldier cautiously crawled up to the edge of the high elevation precipice as if he were doing surveillance on a rebel camp. The view that greeted him was awe inspiring. Thousands of ridges and river carved valleys stretched out for hundreds of miles in all directions. From Lion's Bluff, Wilder could see the rolling green hills of East Tennessee, the ridges of western Virginia and the distant peaks of Kentucky. Many of the mountains to his west overlooked the hallowed ground of old battlefields and forgotten skirmishes. The summer sun sank towards distant Tennessee valleys as the veteran General sat on Lion's Bluff in quiet reflection. With his feet stretched out and his back wedged between two large rocks, Wilder watched the sun slowly disappear beneath him. It was the first time he ever looked down at a sunset.

In the shadows of dusk, John Wilder hiked back towards camp. His mind felt cleansed from the worries and schemes of life. The smell of cherry wood smoke indicated that the camp site was near. Shell had prepared new potatoes, corn on the cob and a brace of freshly shot grouse for supper. With a meal sufficient for a working man, Wilder stretched out on a quilt and propped his head on a rolled up saddle blanket. As he looked up at the stars, the old Yankee General felt one of those rare life moments when one feels stress free. The next day he would be riding back down into civilization to catch a train and negotiate deals with greedy investors, but in that moment the money, status and material aspects of life seemed inconsequential. All that mattered was the sunset and sunrise. All that mattered was getting lost in God's creation. Wilder drifted off to sleep.

At first light, Shell stoked up the campfire to prepare breakfast. John Wilder climbed out of his tent and wandered towards the nearby eastern edge of a dew soaked bald. In the same way he enjoyed looking down at the sunset the evening before, Wilder planned to watch the morning sun break over the ridges.

Looking across the predawn expanse, the General rubbed the sleep out of his eyes. Shell brought over a cup of hot coffee and recalled how the Cherokee would measure one's age by the number of sunrises they got to witness. A thick layer of white fog covered the lower ridges and valleys. From the sea of white fog, a few of the higher mountain tops emerged. The high peaks looked like tiny islands in a white ocean. As the sun gleamed over the eastern horizon, the lower ridge tops began to peak out of the receding mist eventually leaving the valleys shrouded in lakes of fog. The morning was glorious to behold. On that first visit to the place that the old mountaineers called "Cloudland," the refreshed General felt a connection to the mountain that would eventually link him to its history. As camp broke and final preparations were made for the trek down the mountain, Wilder knew he would return.

Chapter 2:

The Cloudland Hotel

"Cloudland is most appropriately named, for it is truly a land among the clouds."

-Southern Standard, Tennessee (1887)

A fter his first trip up the mountain, General John Wilder vowed to return. For Wilder to establish a foothold in the land of the clouds, he needed to acquire property. The major landowners of the Roan Highlands in 1870, according to Mitchell County, North Carolina deed books, were the Avery's, Ayers', Burleson's, Edwards', Freemans', Holder's, Hughes', Ledford's and Peakes'. In the 1870s, public documents show that Wilder purchased approximately 46,000 acres of land that spanned from Buladean across the Roan Highlands to present day Avery County. Wilder used quit claim deeds to signify ownership on a large portion of the Roan. Different from a general warranty deed which must have a clear title and specific boundaries, a quit claim deed does not require a chain of title but only shows a transfer has taken place. As a result, quit claim deeds are sometimes used to purchase land that has an unclear title or survey. Whether or not Wilder's title was clear cannot be proven, but Mitchell records show in 1877 that Wilder quit claimed 46,000 acres on top of Roan Mountain. Being a risk taker, Wilder may have decided to use adverse possession to acquire some of his land.

Wilder initially built a twenty room log cabin on top of Roan Mountain. Because the house could not hold all his family, friends and associates, Wilder decided to build the luxurious Cloudland

In the *Shadow* of the
ROAN

Hotel. The mountain top resort had 268 rooms with majestic views into North Carolina and Tennessee. The hotel also included a ten pin bowling alley and stable. The cost to stay at the Cloudland was $2.50 per day and was advertised to be well worth the price "especially for those with hay fever." Meals were included with the fee and said by many of the guests to be the best ever served at a summer resort hotel. Visitors to the Cloudland were typically wealthy and educated. Though the hotel registry has not been found, it was said that guests included British royalty, high-profile wealthy industrialists, academics and politicians.

The large white hotel could be seen for hundreds of miles on a clear day or totally disappear into passing clouds. In late spring, visitors watched the lush green grasses of the vast balds dance to cool breezes. In summer, the temperate high-elevation climate served to provide natural air conditioning for the hotel and its visitors. In mid-June, guests often reclined on the Cloudland's long porches and enjoyed viewing endless acres of the largest natural rhododendron bloom in the world. A sea of pink flowers framed by grassy balds and the deep green hues of the evergreen forests made the experience unforgettable. As the pedals of the rhododendrons faded, the heat of summer ushered in another entertaining natural event. On hot evenings, spectators gathered on the rooftop of the hotel to watch thunderheads build in the Tennessee Valley. When the conditions were perfect, the shadows of dusk ushered in an awe-inspiring light show for the Cloudland's visitors. Distant lightning storms flashed and streaked through the evening sky. From the four story vantage point of the highest hotel east of the Rockies, wealthy guests admired God's fireworks well into the night. In July of 1887, the Tennessee Press Association met at the Cloudland Hotel for their annual meeting. For many of the reporters, it was their first trip to the land of the clouds. The writer described the Cloudland and briefly mentioned the thunderstorms in an article entitled "Among the Clouds."

The Cloudland Hotel operated on top Roan Mountain from 1885 to around 1907. During the summer months, guests would escape to the mountain retreat for fine lodging and breathtaking views. Photo Courtesy Library of Congress. (1905)

AMONG THE CLOUDS.
MEETING OF THE TENNESSEE PRESS ASSOCIATION AT CLOUDLAND HOTEL.

Gorgeous Mountain Scenery Which No Pen Can Describe.

Cloudland Hotel is located on the top of Roan Mountain, in Mitchell County, NC, and Carter County, TN, the state line passing through the hotel. It is reached by taking the East Tennessee, Virginia and Georgia Railway to Johnson City, and from that point the East Tennessee and Western North Carolina Railroad to Roan Mountain station, a distance of 25 miles, and from thence 12 miles in hacks or on horseback up the side of Roan Mountain to the hotel. No pen can adequately describe the magnificent scenery along the narrow gauge railroad from Johnson City, up the Doe River Gorge, or the soul-inspiring views to be seen from the sides and summits of Roan Mountain and neighboring peaks. The train which carried the press party, about fifty in number, from Johnson City, was composed of the

The Cloudland was marketed to guests as the highest human habitation east of the Rocky Mountains. The full brochure outlined pricing and sites around Roan Mountain. Photo Courtesy of UNC Chapel Hill Archive. (1900)

mail and baggage car, two coaches, and an open observation car. A number of other excursionists were also aboard, and the train was well filled. Doe river canyon is four miles long and 1500 feet deep. The mind grows tired at the very thought of trying to describe the wild grandeur of the scenery along this wonderful road. As the train toils

View from the site of the Cloudland Hotel looking into North Carolina. Wealthy guests would tour the numerous overlooks and trails surrounding the luxurious hotel during the summer months. Photo by Allen Cook. (View from Cloudland Site, 2019)

laboriously up the steep grades, plunging through dark tunnels, spanning deep chasms, or hugging the mountain in short curves above dizzy heights, with the rock-ribbed mountains towering hundreds of feet above in almost perpendicular walls on the other side, one feels painfully the utter incapacity of the mind to so group words and phrases to fittingly describe the varied, grand and picturesque beauty of the place. On one side the eye sweeps over a vast mountain steep rearing its head into the clouds, while upon the other the Doe River leaps, foams and roars through the rocks and dense shades hundreds of feet below. The press party reached Roan Mountain Station about half past eight o'clock, Wednesday morning, July 13th. Eight large hacks and about twenty saddle horses were in waiting to convey the party to Cloudland. Some four or five of the horsemen pushed ahead, and reached Cloudland a few minutes past twelve o'clock. The writer secured a good saddle horse, and in company with Maj. II. C. Bate, made the journey up the mountain in little more than five hours, reaching Cloudland at 2:15 p.m. The party stopped for an hour at noon, and had lunch by the roadside. All of the hacks reached Cloudland Hotel shortly after four o'clock, and the crowd soon began to scatter over the mountain to the many advantageous places for views.

The hotel can accommodate between four and five hundred guests, is three stories high, with long verandas on two sides. The peculiar directions of the state line between North Carolina and Tennessee gets one considerably confused in geography. It is generally supposed that North Carolina lies east of Tennessee, yet the eastern end of Cloudland Hotel is in Tennessee, while the western end is in North Carolina. In the Tennessee side of the house you are surrounded on three sides by North Carolina, and in the North Carolina side you are surrounded on three sides by Tennessee. The two states are hooked together something like the manner of a patent car coupler, making three parallel state lines for a short distance, across the center one of which the hotel is built. The hotel building, ten pin alley and stables contain 1,500,000 feet of lumber, all of which was cut by a small saw mill near the hotel, from the small pine trees growing on the mountain, which averages only sixty feet of lumber to the tree. Everything about the building is scrupulously clean, the rooms are all neatly furnished and altogether it is a delightfully pleasant, comfortable homelike place. The guests are most bountifully fed, the tables being the best we have ever found at a summer resort hotel.

With a favorable condition of the atmosphere one can look upon seven different states from the summit of Roan Mountain, and the eye looks over range after range of mountains covering a territory of 50,000 square miles. The rock formations of Roan Mountain show it to be the oldest part of the continent, and according to scientific theories it reared its lofty peaks up into space centuries before the Alps emerged from the depths of the sea. Here the geologist,

.....**Rates of Board**.....

Per day, ... $ 2.00 to $ 2.50
Per week, . . . 10.00 to 15.00

Children under ten years of age, in children's ordinary, one-half rate.

Children occupying seats in main dining room to the exclusion of other guests, full rates.

White servants, three-fourths rate.

Colored servants, in colored servants' quarters, one-half rate.

.....**Hack and Baggage Rate**.....

Hack rates, $3.00 for the round trip, and $1.00 each way on trunks. Hand baggage free.

❧ ❧ ❧

The Roan Mountain Hotel...
Roan Mountain, Tenn.

Is run in connection with Cloudland Hotel. Season of 1900 begins June 1st and ends October 15th.

Rates of board, $2.00 per day; $8.00 to $10.00 per week.

A very delightful place to spend the summer months.

Address all communications to

N. L. MURRELL, Proprietor,
Cloudland, Mitchell County,
North Carolina.

In 1900, a guest could spend a night at the Cloudland for $2.50. The above marketing material outlines the rates and details. Photo Courtesy of UNC Chapel Hill Archive. (1900)

mineralogist, and botanist find the most fertile fields for their investigations that are to be found on the globe. Within the bounds of Mitchell County, NC, every mineral known to commerce except coal has been discovered. In this respect it is the most remarkable county in the world. Numerous mica mines are now being worked there, and *every one of them show unmistakable evidences of having been operated by a pre-historic race of people hundreds of years before America was discovered by Columbus.*

The temperature at Cloudland Hotel rarely ever exceeds 70 during the day, and the rarified air makes it seem much cooler than it really is. Big log fires are built up in the parlor and office every evening and morning, and the dining room and halls are all heated by a furnace in the basement. Overcoats and heavy wraps are necessary for the comfort of all who get outside of the building after night. The water used is pure clear freestone, pumped from a large spring near the hotel, its temperature being only fourteen degrees above the freezing point.

The Chicago, Cincinnati and Charleston Railroad, which is now being surveyed, will pass within three miles of Cloudland Hotel. As soon as it is built, Gen. Wilder will construct an incline plane railroad from the hotel to the C. C. & C. road, making a quick all rail route to Cloudland. No one who visits Cloudland once and sees what Gen. Wilder has already accomplished there, will doubt his capacity to carry out anything he may undertake, and it is simply a matter of time until Cloudland hotel will be reached by rail.

Cloudland is most appropriately named, for it is truly a land among the clouds. From the summit of the mountain one or more thunderstorms can be seen driving through the valleys below at almost any hour of the day, and the cloud views every morning and evening are exquisitely beautiful.
-Southern Standard, **Tennessee** (1887)

One important feature of the hotel was its orientation. Being built on the border line between North Carolina and Tennessee, a guest could dine in Tennessee and sleep in North Carolina. In fact, it was said that the state line was drawn on the floor of the Cloudland. Guests could enjoy a glass of the finest wine in Tennessee or soberly lounge in North Carolina. The Cloudland was quite a sight for all the locals and there are still a few old timers (at the time of the original writing of this account) that can remember the hotel in all of its grandeur. If one rides to the top of Roan Mountain, they can see the site of the Cloudland behind the United States Forest Service fee booth.

For many vacationers, the scenery was the most entertaining wonder to observe from the 6,400 feet vantage point. When the leaves turned infinite shades of orange, red, brown and yellow; many guests would ascend to the Cloudland to view the autumn scenery. The visibility of the clear fall days, made autumn a favorite time for guests to spend a week at the ridgetop retreat. The clean air and breathtaking scenery made the Cloudland a top destination for guests. The top rate amenities and exquisite accommodations made them want to stay. Many newspapers of the day described the top rate accommodations of the Cloudland Hotel and the amazing views of Roan Mountain.

A Tramp to Roan Mountain.

Cloudland, July 2. To the Editor of The Lenoir Topic:
Something over two weeks ago I left Lenoir to spend a month or so at Blowing Rock, and while there to take a tramp through the mountains, partly for health, and partly for pleasure. Cloudland Hotel on the summit of Roan Mountain was my objective point, and today after many a weary step, finds me here. While on my tramp I have visited quite a good many places of some interest to the mountain tourist. Among some other places, I have been to Grandfather, Banner Elk, Cranberry, Johnson City, and Roan Mountain Station, which is situated at the base of the Roan, and from which you take the hack for Cloudland, unless you are traveling in the manner in which I am, then you take the road. I left the station this morning at 8 o'clock, and came to the top of the mountain, a distance of twelve and a half miles in 4 3/4 hours.

When I got here I found the hotel, as its name imports, shrouded in the clouds, and to my great surprise, Mr. Editor, it rained nearly all evening. The view of course was entirely shut out. But to my great joy at 5 o'clock in the evening the clouds burst and cleared away, and the sun came out from his dismal abode and made the rising fog and drifting clouds present a hundred hues. I will not attempt to describe the scene that lay before me, presenting every variety of mountain scenery, from the most delicate flower and threadlike streamlet, to the cloud that lies in golden folds along the horizon of the setting sun and the lofty mountain summit that hides itself in the clouds. If I were to attempt to describe it, I would say that it is eminently grand.

The hotel is large, and has a capacity to accommodate 500 guests. It is built entirely of native balsam except the window frames and sash which were brought from Minnesota. The top of the Roan is treeless and is set in grass which is from 4 to 6 inches high, affording pasturage for quite a large herd of horses and cattle. This pasture is 6 or 8 miles long, and is fenced by the timber line alone. The hotel table is supplied with beef from these cattle, and it is the fattest and sweetest meat in the world. The hotel is connected with the hotel at Roan Mountain Station by telephone, and you can converse with a friend 12 miles away. General Wilder, the proprietor, is absent on a business trip to Chattanooga, Tennessee, but his son-in-law, Mr. Stratton is acting in his place. He is accommodating, and pleasing in his manner, and immediately on arriving makes you feel quite at home.

I will remain all night and in the morning I will reluctantly take my leave; and I will say, in taking my departure, farewell, king of the Alleghenies, no mountain trip is complete without embracing thee! TRAMP.
-The Lenoir Topic, **North Carolina** (1886)

The furnishings of the Cloudland Hotel were the best of the era. New spring beds were standard in all the rooms. Locally made quilts served to provide warmth in the cool high altitude air. Every room was equipped with a wash stand, bowl and pitcher. There are a few old timers who live in the valley that possess white china wash bowls and pitchers from the Cloudland. The hotel's floor plan provided one indoor bathroom which was located on the level above the basement near the barber shop and office. The bath tub was framed with balsam and lined with copper. Each room had one window and a lockable

View from the Sunset Rock on top of Roan Mountain. The Sunset Rock was a favorite destination for visitors to the Cloudland. Photo By Allen Cook. (2019).

door. The dressers were locally made from cherry wood and old chestnut trees logged from the valleys near the Roan. The floors of the guest rooms were carpeted and neatly kept. The hotel was heated by a furnace in the basement. Since Wilder made his fortune in the furnace business, he used the latest technology of the day to heat the Cloudland. Other notable features of the hotel included the basement which functioned as a kindergarten classroom and a dance floor. The location on the ground level served to keep down noise and also provided a well-insulated area, shielded from the sub-zero winter winds.

Bakersville Enterprise: *Part of the roof of the Cloudland Hotel was blown off last week by a high wind. Gen. Wilder is up there this week having it repaired in order to open the house by June 1st.*
-*The Wilmington Messenger*, North Carolina (1894)

In the *Shadow* of the
ROAN

The winds atop Roan Mountain would often gust to speeds over 80 miles per hour. Wind driven clouds and rain permeated the wood structure and caused rot. Forceful gusts of wind also frequently damaged the structure. As a result, maintenance and repair to the resort was a constant task and prohibitive cost. Roan Mountain winters took their toll on the Cloudland and in the early 1900s the once fancy resort began to decline. In 1907, the Cloudland ceased operation as a high elevation destination resort. In the article, *Mountain Climb into the Cloudland*, the writer described the condition of the hotel in the year 1909.

MOUNTAIN CLIMB INTO CLOUDLAND
Regal Pleasure Related in a Royal Way
A TRIP UP THE ROAN
The Air Was So Fresh and So Full of Ozone, the Way Was Varied at Every Turn, the Trees So Grand that Mountain Climbing Was a Joy.
To the Editor: "Report by four thirty at the depot," was the order given to those at Spruce Pine contemplating a trip to the Roan on the morrow. The plan was to run down the "Clinchfield Route" to Toecane, drive up to Bakersville, spend the night, and in the early morning make the climb.

At the hour appointed, our little group of four, Rev. William Black, Mrs. Black, Miss Bessie McCord, and myself, beguiled the time jesting over the imagined ordeals of the day just ahead. Soon, however, we were swinging around well-graded curves by rocks, waterfalls, rhododendron and rugged mountain sides along the Toe in a region so long shut off from the rest of the State. Now the vestibule - train has supplanted the mountain wagon. Outlet for a great land is made by the Carolina, Clinchfield and Ohio Railroad and, at the same time, another summering place opened up for those who dwell in the flat lands of the lower latitudes. Too soon the delightful ride came to an end with the call, "All out for Toecane." (This is near the confluence of the Toe River and Cane Creek, hence the name).

The drive of three miles up Cane Creek to Bakersville is not without interest to a crowd off on a frolic. The rippling waters of the creek, the farms on edge with corn and grass necessarily clinging close to the soil, the eager-eyed children by cottage door give variety to the monotonous jolting of a road at times in the bed of the creek, then on the bank, or else rising to the crest of a ridge for the regal pleasure of descending once more to rock-bottom. The good natured driver, black as midnight, with teeth of pearl, responded freely to all questions, wise and otherwise. Off to the north of the sunset was the Roan, as it had stood for centuries, grim and silent and eternal. In the losing moment, of this eager afternoon, a kind of unearthly splendor hungover the lofty summit creating a fresh anxiety for the dawn of a new day.

A cordial welcome at Young's Hotel, an ample supper for mountain appetites, arrangements made for horses sure of foot, and the assurance of early breakfast given, left nothing to be desired but a good night's sleep. All was propitious. The September night was fine; the landscape breathed repose; the air gave hints of coming frost, a full moon was in the sky; the stars spoke peace; and Bakersville was silent as a deserted village. So, lights were out before nine. The moments flew, seemingly not an hour had passed till the shrill voice of some early cock set a hundred throats to the task of heralding the grey dawn. Soon all were astir, alert and eager, congratulating each the other on the fine night for rest. However, one discordant note was heard, from the young lady of the party who had spent much of the night in the fine pastime of mounting horses, falling over cliffs jumping chasms and climbing cataracts.

Breakfast over, the mount sufficient for Mr. B. J. Young, our guide, Mrs. Hyams and Mr. Baily, who had joined us, was at the door. Six good mountain climbers guaranteed to reach cloudland and to return all safely stood ready. Mrs. Hyams sat with ease on Clipper, Miss Bessie mounted Doc, Honest John was assigned Mr. Black, I rode Colonel, while our guide led the way on Pioneer. A degree of pride was ours in having a pilot first on the Roan more than half a century

31

ago, now found making the trip only on special occasions.

Just as the sun began to gild the upper slopes, through the frosty air under a cloudless sky the jolly group cantered away up the rough mountain road. All got well settled to the saddle on the first four miles of gradual ascent. We rode face to face with the balsam-covered slopes, the way ever growing steeper as the road lost itself in a narrow trail. The climb was on now in earnest. But the air was so fresh and full of ozone, the way so varied at every turn, the forest's trees so grand, and the vegetation such a rich green that we were oblivious to the rest of the world. A shady nook here, a tiny waterfall there, some marvelous formation around the bend lured us on. Sugar maples, chestnuts and oaks lifted their giant forms to the sky while ferns and mosses reveled in their shadows. Summer held high carnival but the scarlet and gold on the early leaf betokened coming autumn and the storm-king's reign. Incidents by the way were not without passing interest. A herd of sleek, fat cattle free from flies and mosquitoes, capering on the steeps told of life rich and full; the yellow-jackets putting springs in our horses excited no little merriment; and the familiar airs sung by two rich full voices rose, swelled and swept over the valley below adding zest to the climb. One of the group lined over the long gone years and was rich in incident and anecdote.

Later, however, the trivial and commonplace failed to interest, for with every additional angle more peaks greeted the vision and a new world was created below and around us. On and up, we pushed. The panorama widened, the tints and shadings deepened, and mountains multiplied. The failing vegetation, trees dwarf in size, and ever increasing rocks indicated near approach to the "ball ground." Alder bushes with every appearance of being singed, scrubby balsam, heather, and rocks, are the chief products of these upper altitudes. Now the climb is on in all its glory. Each pause to rest jaded steeds is filled with exclamations over the beatific vision to the east. Finally, we reach the summit of the ridge, tie our horses and clamber up to Sion's bluff. From the "observatory" lie in full view the world and its glory. A billowy sea of purple mountains rolls away to every point of the compass. Mitchell, Table Rock, Haw's Bill, Grandfather and other noted peaks are on or below a horizontal line from our vantage ground. To wait and wonder and worship under the blue depths becomes the mood. Fields, farms, roads, cottages, hamlets, streams and mountains in their abundance tend to bewilder. Only noted peaks and objects near gain the attention.

From Sion's Bluff the precipitous cliff drops hundreds of feet and the land falls away to the west until a chasm nearly four thousand feet deep yawns before the eye. This opens out into a wide valley allowing a current of air to sweep up over the bluff sufficient ordinarily to return tossed over hats and coats and shawls. But this calm morning a leaf would have gone down. Mr. Young said not in fifty years had he seen so light a breeze at this point. Undisturbed, the sky wore its deepest blue and the soft haze swept a wide horizon. The ethereal splendor about the still solemn mountain top above man's little rounds gave slight hint of earth's commonplace.

You see into seven states from the Roan, as claimed, may not be possible. I should not care to venture an assertion. Certainly, if such is, our eyes rested on the full quota for none could be favored with a more propitious day. Be that as it may, this much is true: A new sense of ownership comes to one having a foot each in North Carolina and Tennessee, with the eye permitted to sweep such a vast expanse of valley, mountain and sky. Something in the atmosphere adds to the joy of this pleasing sense of proprietorship. In riding along the open crest, the temperature and air inhaled remind one of the parks of high altitudes in Colorado.

The Cloudland Hotel, which began business in 1885, and enjoyed prosperity for years, has not been opened for two seasons. The increase expense of operating has become prohibitive. A family remains up there the year round providing food and provender for parties spending a short while. Three months in summer are glorious for the tourist, but the winter brings another tale. When that mother of fourteen children tells of their life, the splendor fades like the mists from the mountain-tops, or rather, the horror settles down on one like the billows of fog and snow that roll up over the Roan when a blizzard is on.

A drink of the clear, cold, spring water six thousand feet above sea, observations from Sion's Bluff, North observatory, and Sunrise Rock, gathering balsam for pillows, (what woman would return without this treasure?), dinner, with an hour's rest to follow, on a perch six thousand three hundred and ninety-four feet above sea level are enough to fill full the glorious hours.

San Francisco makes much of Mount Tamalpais overlooking the Pacific, the city, Sacramento Valley, and a sea of hills and mountains, but, to me, this view is far superior. Some like it better than Pike's Peak and are sure it surpasses Mitchell, for the crowding of other peaks do not allow the same sweep of vision and that sense of "aboveness," though Mitchell is about three hundred feet higher.

Of the hair-breadth escapes on the return, the moving accidents over cliff and scare of the fair young drummer, and the efforts to ride into the village fresh and debonair, I shall write after Bakersville has grasped its opportunity and become a popular resort with the climb to Cloudland, its most popular side-trip.
M. T. PLYLER. Washington, N. C., Sept. 18.
-*The Farmer and Mechanic,* North Carolina (1909)

At the time of the article in *The Farmer and Mechanic*, the Cloudland had been closed for two seasons. Simply put, the Cloudland Hotel did not make money. It was not a lucrative enterprise for several reasons. First, the economy took a downturn causing General Wilder to lose much of his wealth during the early 1900s. As a result, the Cloudland did not have Wilder's funds to bankroll maintenance and other expenses. Another hindrance to the old hotel was the upkeep of the roads that led to the Roan. The steep and winding mountain roads were bumpy and often eroded due to the many horses and wagons that would access the hotel. The final factor that led to the demise of

The Waites Ledford Homeplace was said to have trim and siding that was taken from the Cloudland Hotel. Note the trim and posts. Photo By Allen Cook. (2019)

the Cloudland was the long winter months of inaccessibility. There were only four months that guests could visit the hotel with any assurance of a temperate stay. Due to the long off-season, revenues were nearly non-existent. The off-season months of cold weather coupled with difficult access limited the hotel to being only a seasonal venue.

Depreciation took its toll on the once fine Cloudland resort. Continuous maintenance and profitability issues made the hotel a losing business venture. Eventually, the salvage rights to the hotel were sold and the building materials were auctioned to the surrounding local residents. Once the locals saw that Wilder was gone, they began to depreciate the hotel as well. Not wanting the fine cherry, native fir and chestnut lumber sawn from their properties to go to waste, they salvaged unsold building materials from the hotel. When looking at many of the old houses that are still around today,

The Wilt Ledford House at the head of Charles Creek Road was made from the Cloudland Hotel. The old fir siding bears nail holes where it was removed from the old hotel. Photo By Allen Cook. (2006)

one can still see fancy moldings and fir siding that used to be on the Cloudland Hotel. On the head of Charles Creek Road in the nearby community of Glen Ayre, my Grandpa Charlie Ledford told of the Cloudland's lumber that was repurposed in the construction of the Waites and Wilt Ledford homes. To this day, one can still see pieces of the Cloudland's trim that lines the porch of the Waites Ledford homeplace. The Wilt Ledford house was also made from the Cloudland Hotel. Faded white paint and old nail holes reveal the siding had been torn off the Cloudland and used in the old home. The seasoned fir siding is a beautiful gray color and the wood is naturally bug proof.

In addition to lumber, many residents of both Glen Ayre and Roaring Creek hold antiques that were taken from the Cloudland. Old timer Cleo Edwards owned a bedside water pot that was used in the rooms of the Cloudland. Old beds and furniture bought or salvaged from the mountain top resort still hide in the backs of barns and old houses

Marker at site of the Cloudland Hotel on top of Roan Mountain. Photo By Allen Cook. (2019)

surrounding the Roan to this day. Many residents in Roan Mountain and Burbank, Tennessee still hold Cloudland memorabilia as well.

Eventually, the Wilder property was sold to the Reynolds Corporation and finally to the U.S. Government. When the U.S. Forest Service acquired the land, they bulldozed the remains of the hotel and made a parking area adjacent to the old hotel site. Today, a marker is all that remains to mark the site where the Cloudland once stood.

General John Wilder is linked with a brief and interesting chapter in Roan Mountain's long history. After his first trip to the Roan, Wilder purchased the top of the mountain and opened it to tourism. The endless views and temperate clean air energized all those who visited Wilder's ridge top retreat. Wilder's four story luxury hotel interrupted the ridgeline of Roan Mountain for over a quarter of a century. During that time, the Cloudland made a lasting impression on the people who visited and the locals in the surrounding valleys.

Entrance to Cloudland Hotel Site on Roan Mountain.
Photo By Allen Cook. (2019)

Chapter 3:

Glen Ayre, NC in the Early 1900s

"The contrast is as different as sunshine is from clouds when it comes to making a comparison to Little Rock Creek and Oak Hill. There is no sitting on the outside talking about bulls, boars and rams for such is the case among certain Charles Creek people. Yes, it seems like something out of ordinary things to see a class of old men singing and taking part in Sunday School."

-Letter from Glen Ayre Resident, William Ingle *(1921)*

Mountain fields have slowly reverted to forest over the last 100 years and now hide crumbled rock foundations of home sites that once stood along the creek bottoms and hollows of Glen Ayre, North Carolina. The small mountain community lies in the shadow of the Roan. Back then, if one stood on top of Roan Mountain and looked down on the valleys of Glen Ayre, they would have seen mostly pasture land with a few woodlots on the steepest terrain. There were many houses in the numerous alpine meadows, more than at the present time. Framed by the Roan, Little Yellow and Hawk Mountains, Glen Ayre encompasses the headwaters of Little Rock Creek. As a result, many locals refer to Glen Ayre as Little Rock Creek. There were several grist mills along Little Rock Creek and at the heads of some of the tributaries was the

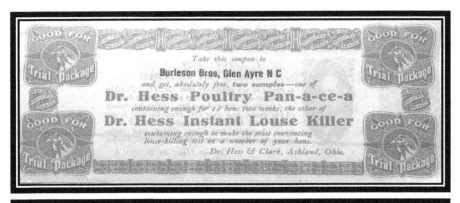

Burleson Brothers Store was located at the convergence of Little Rock Creek and Green Creek. This letterhead is dated from 1907. Also note the coupon for use at Burleson Brothers for free samples of louse killer for poultry. Photo - Allen Cook.

occasional moonshine still. The bottom land was plowed with oxen or draft horses and usually planted in corn and potatoes. The stores were a gathering place for locals to get provisions and exchange opinions. Schools were built every mile or so along the roads that linked the communities. Contrary to stereotypical beliefs, education was available in the mountains. Early schools were commonly located in the community church. Speaking of churches, each mountain settlement had at least one church. Glen Ayre had several churches. Being equipped with a general knowledge of the physical features on the southeastern slopes of Roan Mountain, a more focused account of the area surrounding Glen Ayre reveals interesting facts about the structure of the growing community.

Because of its population and orientation, Glen Ayre held an important position in the early development of Mitchell County. In order to describe the features of the Glen Ayre Community at the turn of the century, one must be able to put themselves in a different frame of mind and try to picture scenes of wagons and dirt roads. Just over a century ago, Glen Ayre was a bustling little community with an economy centered on mining, forestry, and farming. The road to Bakersville did not follow its present route, but rather followed along the Green Creek Valley and then over Rock Creek Pass where it skirted adjacent to the Young Cove. From the Young Cove, the wagon trail connected with Bakersville. Glen Ayre was also linked to Roaring Creek, which is now in Avery County, by a trail that went across the Grassy Ridge and Little Yellow Mountain Pass. To the west, another trail traced the banks of Little Rock Creek and connected Fork Mountain with the road to Bakersville. The presence of several roads merging together made Glen Ayre an ideal place to settle and a lucrative place for a business.

General Stores

If there is one feature of the Glen Ayre Community that has not succumbed to the progress of time, it would have to be the general stores. Although there were a greater number of stores 125 years ago, the ones that have survived through the decades have not changed very much. While some of the establishments still serve as a place for people to socialize and discuss community politics, most general stores are no longer in operation.

Near the convergence of Little Rock Creek and Green Creek was the establishment of Burleson Brothers General Store. The business, owned by Nat and Lafayette Burleson, served the surrounding community with everything from cattle feed to overalls. Lafayette "Fate" Burleson was sheriff of Mitchell County from 1914 to around 1920. Due to this fact, Fate's brother Nathaniel "Nat" Burleson took over the store as part owner. In 1930, Burleson Brothers was sold for $3,000 to William Ford Greene. The store has been passed through the generations to the present owner, Dwight Thomas, who operates the business today. During the days of ownership by Nat and Fate Burleson, Burleson Brothers General Store had a front door that faced towards the Green Creek. When the state constructed highway 261, the front door was situated to face the newly made road. With the exception of some interior modifications and gas pumps, the actual building has not changed very much.

If walls could talk, those in Thomas Grocery could write a best seller. During the store's 100+ years of operation, it has watched young men rise to prominence and hard times cause family fortunes to fall. The general store was the backyard stage where a young man named Steve Ledford first brought his fiddling tunes to the community and then later on to Nashville where he played with various musicians and even appeared at the Grand Ole Opry.

Burleson Brothers was also the site of a killing. Some old timers say that it is haunted by the spirit of Anderson Burleson who was knifed at the store in 1907. As a child, I was told that there was a puddle of blood at the site of the killing that could not be removed by the store keeper. Because it looked unsightly and reminded everyone of the knifing that took place at the establishment, the owner, Fate Burleson constructed a shelf over the spot to hide the gruesome reminder. The fixture served to hide the crimson stained planks from the sight of those who wandered into the store and, as a result, caused the oddity to slowly fade in the passage of time. The few grizzled mountaineers who remember how Fate scrubbed and sanded those cherry boards know that under an old shelf, the blood of Anderson Burleson still cries out for revenge.

Located in the same area as Burleson Brothers Store, J.C. Ayers had a business on the Green Creek. The dual existence of the stores bred competition which kept both establishments' prices low. The location of the store was near the old post office and Glen Ayre Baptist Church. There were also several grist mills along Little Rock Creek which sold cornmeal and flour to the local residents. The Ayers store sold hardware and food products that were picked up from the train

The S.C. Miller Store (Top) was said to have been near the present-day property of the Steve Miller Hidden Creek Office in Glen Ayre. The J.C. Ayers Dry Goods Store (Middle) was located near Green Creek Road in Glen Ayre, NC. The D.M. Cook & Greene Store (Bottom) was located along present-day Fork Mountain Road. Photo - Allen Cook.

depot in Toecane. Receipts show that clothing was also sold at J.C. Ayers General Store. The population of the Glen Ayre Community and proximity to major roads allowed for both Burleson Brothers and

J.C. Ayers general stores to be profitable.

Other stores that existed in the early part of the century were scattered along the banks of Little Rock Creek. At the bottom of the Gouge Cove Creek was the Claude McEntire Store. In Fork Mountain the D.M. Cook & Greene business would provide customers with dry goods. In Roan Valley, near present day Roan Valley Baptist Church, was the J.M. Ayers General Store. The S.C. Miller Store was also in Glen Ayre and I suspect it to be where the Steve Miller, Hidden Creek office is presently situated. In the early 1900's, there were at least five stores along a two mile stretch within the Glen Ayre community. Because transportation was slower and less mechanized, every community had a place that conveniently sold goods to the surrounding people. When the highways became paved, the community stores began to fade in the passage of progress. Presently, Thomas Grocery is the only general store still operating in Glen Ayre.

Schools

There were four school districts in the communities beneath Roan Mountain. Near the road to Bakersville in the settlement of Glen Ayre was the Little Rock Creek School. The building consisted of a one room log cabin situated on the banks of the creek near present day Little Rock Creek Baptist Church.

In the early 1900s, church services and school classes were held in the same building. The Glen Ayre District included students that were residing from Burleson Creek to the head of the Green Creek. Up to 1923, all the schools of Mitchell County were supported by the churches and drew their funds from the home mission board of the Southern Baptist Association. In 1901, there were 124 pupils attending the school in Glen Ayre. Adjacent to the northeastern border of the Little Rock Creek School District, was the Roan Valley School District. It was situated on the Milton Young house site which is now near the present day property owned by the Cox family. This district covered land from the Charles Creek to the top of Roan Mountain. Roan Valley had 94 pupils that attended the school on a

The old Glen Ayre School House is still standing to this day. Located near Burleson Creek in Glen Ayre, NC; the old rock building served students through the 1950s. Letterhead from Glen Ayre Graded School and Roan Mountain High School are pictured below. Photos By Allen Cook. (1997)

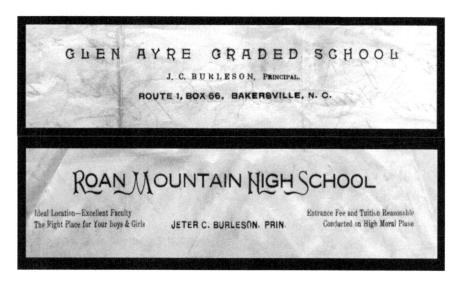

regular basis. The lower two districts that lay beneath Roan Mountain were Fork Mountain and the Burleson District. The Fork Mountain School which served students from Cook Town Creek to Rock Dale, educated 114 students in a building where Bethlehem Baptist Church now stands. Burleson school district covered the area from Gouge Hollow to Cook Town creek. The school building was located at the bottom of the Gouge Cove Creek on the present-day property of Sherrill Burleson, and serviced 83 pupils. All the schools were operated by funds generated through local taxes. The four schools had a combined total of 415 children in attendance, evidencing the higher amount of people settled in the area beneath the Roan. In 1922, the four schools were consolidated by Mitchell County for reasons that are unclear. Citizens residing in outlying areas did not like the idea of consolidation because the children would have to endure long rides to the central school. After much controversy concerning the location and transportation to the new school, plans were approved for a site bordering Burleson Creek. The new consolidated school was called the Glen Ayre School House and operated until the 1960s. The building can still be seen as one drives up Highway 261 in Glen Ayre.

Churches
The final feature I will discuss in the early life of the Glen Ayre Community was the churches. The prominent church of the area was the Little Rock Creek Baptist Church. The earliest deed shows the

Photograph taken in front of the Little Rock Creek Baptist Church. Back row standing left to right: Rev. Huey Buchanan, Reggie Edwards, Aught Burleson, Walt Gouge, Fate or Charlie Holder, Coy Holder, Hugh Buchanan, Cling Ledford, Mr. Childers, Clarence Buchanan, Charlie McIntuff, Joe Mills, Charlie Ward. Fifth row: Millie Buchanan, Mae Randolph, Stokes Ledford, James Gouge, John Randolph, Harry Mosely, Doc Ayers, Floyd Thomas, Earnest Gouge (beside column, right). Hersh Burleson in front of left column. Fourth row: Edith McIntuff, Gracie Biddix, Ruth Gouge, Maude Miller, Tilda Burleson, Carrie Burleson, Lucy Burleson, Greenlee Holders daughter with child, Dan Wilcox, Steve Park, Greenlee Holder. Third row: Luther Ward, Ford Greene, Floyd McCurry, Mae Ward Burleson, Dorthy Gouge, Pearl Buchanan, Ethel Burleson, Tilda Burleson, Anne Miller, Arlee Ellis. Second Row: Ralph Burleson, Maude Burleson, Merrill Burleson, Irene Burleson, Doris Ledford, Carl Gouge, Judy Buchanan, John Childers, Ruby Burleson, Ned Burleson, Junior Childers, Thelma Lamb, Ora Burleson, Ed Miller, Charles Burleson. Front row: Thelma Lamb, Marie Ledford, unknown. Photo – Janie Ledford Cook.

building was constructed around 1892. The original church was built on the Green Creek side of Little Rock Creek and also served as a school.

Much to Pastor S.M. Greene's dismay and the school kids' pleasure, the building was destroyed in the 1900 May flood. After the flood, the church was reconstructed on its present site which is opposite the Green Creek. The new chapel housed 173 members and the pastor received $12 per year for preaching. The founding deacons of 1892 as listed on the deed for construction were J.G. Burleson, S.J. Buchanan, J.A. Buchanan and Joseph Greene. In 1907, the pastor was S.D. Tipton and the church had 205 members as stated in the minutes of the 1907 North Carolina Baptist Convention. Other Baptist churches in the community were Burleson Chapel near the Gouge Cove Creek (same building as Burleson School) which held 91 members and Fork Mountain Baptist Church with Pastor L.H. Greene's 136 members. Roan Valley Baptist Church was shown to exist in 1880 but did not keep any records in the association minutes (they may have been combined with Little Rock Creek's minutes). At the site of the present day Apostolic Church in Glen Ayre, was the Methodist Episcopal Chapel. The Methodist later combined membership with the Little Rock Creek Baptist Church and the old building later became the Apostolic Church House.

With the churches specified, a closer examination reveals the typical Sunday service experience. Upon finding an old letter comparing a church in Oak Hill, West Virginia to the Little Rock Creek Baptist Church in Glen Ayre, the differences were somewhat humorous:

August 14, 1921

To: Jeter Burleson
From: William Ingle

We have arrived here all right...I have attended Sabbath School today at the Baptist Church in Oak Hill. The school is certainly a fine one. The building is large and commodious, having stained glass in the windows and being well furnished inside having the appearance of having been built by a Rockefellow or a Carnige. The seats are arranged in semicircle form; just like the seats in Congress, it puts me in mind of the House of Representatives.

The good part is to see so many people at Sunday school. There was something like between 300 or 400 people in the classes. Everyone took part in the singing. The old men were in their classes and took part in the singing too. You might well imagine some music where 400 people is all singing and well taught in such music.

The contrast is as different as sunshine is from clouds when it comes to making a comparison to Little Rock Creek and Oak Hill. There is no sitting on the outside talking about bulls, boars, and rams for such is the case among certain Charles Creek people. Yes, it seems like something out of ordinary things to see a class of old men singing and taking part in Sunday School. Yes, you might meet up with these Charles Creek people fifty times and there talk is ever the same old subject - the domestic animals that I have just mentioned. I have not halfway described the church building here. Its beauty is far in excess of the Little Rock Creek Baptist Church...

The churches today do not have as many members as 75 years ago because the populations are not as high in the mountain area. The messages preached back then often had a theme centered on salvation through faith in the virgin birth, crucifixion and resurrection of Jesus Christ. It was not uncommon to hear sermons based on the themes of the early American preacher, Jonathan Edwards' message, "Sinners in the Hands of an Angry God." The mountain churches often required members to refrain from sinful activities. Wayward church members would get temporarily expelled or "churched" for not exhibiting moral behavior. Church records show that some of my ancestors were churched for "frolicking." My Great Grandma always said that a praying knee and a dancing foot can't be on the same leg. Minutes also show how other members were often expelled for "partaking of intoxicating spirits." Even though members would get churched, they would often be welcomed back into fellowship if they renounced and turned away from their wrongs. Through the lens of today, the mountain churches may seem legalistic but back then, most mountain people respected straight talk and appreciated the fact that churches upheld a high moral standard. In the same manner, most local congregations treasured convicting messages that were God inspired and not lukewarm or "watered" down.

Today, the Glen Ayre Community does not have the same features that it once did in the 1920s. The clear meadows of yesteryear have now reverted to forest and summer homes have been built where old homesteads once stood. The families, however, are firmly rooted into the rocky Roan dirt and many still live on heritage land. With a snapshot of life 100 years ago, many of the old stories that have been collected in this book will now take on an authentic perspective that will better reflect this era in Roan Mountain history.

Glen Ayre and the Mail Order Husband

(Just a funny letter I found while researching)

Everyone has heard about mail order brides. The letter below is from a potential mail order husband. My Great-Great-Grandma Hess Burleson resided in Glen Ayre and received the letter a few years after her husband, Anderson Burleson was killed by the tax collector in a fight over taxes. She never remarried after his untimely death. I guess she was not ready to get herself a "Hoosier."

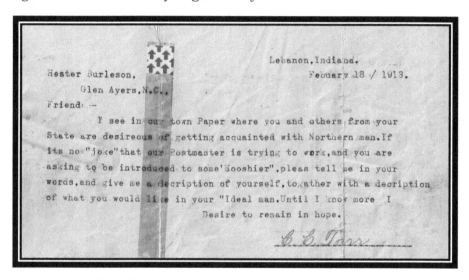

The letter reads as follows:
"Friend:

I see in our town paper where you and others from your state are desireous of getting acquainted with Northern men. If it is no "joke" that our postmaster is trying to work, and you are asking to be introduced to some "Hooshier" pleas(e) tell me in your words, and give me a description of yourself, together with a description of what you would like in your ideal man. Until I know more, I Desire to remain in hope. -BB Tarr"

Chapter 4:
The Killing at Burleson Brothers General Store

"Upon the oath of J. Dosser Burleson, brother to Anderson Burleson, setting forth that J.C. Randolph did on or about the 27th day of June 1907, unlawfully kill and murder one Anderson Burleson, by stabbing him with a knife."

–Mitchell County Court Records (1907)

When my Grandma Ruby Ledford said that my mother, Janie, could have the antique trunk in my Great-Grandfather's barn, I relished the thought of restoring a beautiful heirloom. Ironically, as if my ancestors wanted to be heard, the contents of the trunk seemed to demand more attention than the rusty hinges of the walnut chest. Discovering letters and documents from a man we never knew sparked a curiosity that, until recently, was shrouded in secrecy. As a child I often wondered about the untimely death of my Great-Great-Grandfather William Anderson Burleson. Because the murder was within the community, it was not often discussed among my family. As a result, the life of Anderson needed a final chapter. A chapter that will finally lay to rest the mystery of his brutal death.

The mountain hollows and ridges held people as wild and unique as the meandering streams that flow from atop the Roan. One such person was my Great-Great-Grandfather Anderson Burleson. Born in

Family picture of Anderson Burleson. Anderson was killed at Burleson Brothers Store in 1907. Photo - Allen Cook.

1864 to Reuben and Dorcus Burleson of Glen Ayre, Anderson grew to be an influential figure in Mitchell County. Though he spent most of his life operating a lucrative saw mill beneath Roan Mountain, Burleson also influenced the political climate of the young county. Being seen as trustworthy and honest, Anderson held a good reputation in the community. A member of the International Order of the Odd Fellows (IOOF), a secretive charitable organization geared towards helping orphans, Burleson was an active participant in their many charitable ventures. When the May Flood of 1903 depleted county treasuries, Anderson helped back a loan that was used to assist families devastated by the disaster. He also used his finances to bond

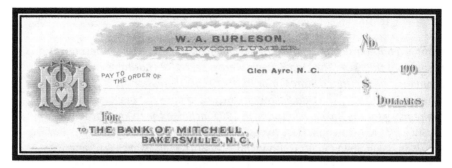

Anderson Burleson operated a sawmill in Glen Ayre, NC. Above is an unused check for W.A. Burleson Hardwood Lumber. Photo - Allen Cook.

public officials and secured other loans which were responsible for the construction of churches and schools. Burleson married Hester Ledford in 1890 and fathered four children in the following years. At the time of his death in 1907, Anderson was 43-years-old. It is at that time I will begin to recollect the events that will close the book on the life of my Great-Great-Grandpa.

When I was a child, my Great Grandfather Aught Burleson would not talk much about the death of his father. All Aught would say was that Anderson was killed with a knife by Jake Randolph in a dispute over taxes. Aught did not discuss any other information concerning the incident probably because he could not recall much of the details surrounding the murder since he was five years old at the time of his daddy's death. As a result, many rumors circulated within the community. I had heard stories from cousins that Anderson was killed by the Ku Klux Klan while walking to Cane Creek, but nothing seemed to add up. Finally, the truth surfaced when my mother, Janie Ledford Cook found the old court documents in the Bakersville Courthouse.

The date of the altercation was June 27, 1907. While Anderson and his cousin, Wylie Clingman Burleson were sitting and talking at Burleson Brothers General Store, now Thomas Grocery, the topic of

Right is a photograph of the Bakersville Odd Fellows. Anderson Burleson was a member of the IOOF. The Odd Fellows were a secretive charitable organization prominent in the United States prior to the Great Depression. This photo was taken prior to 1907. The Odd Fellows in the photo have not been identified but the registry for the Bakersville Lodge in 1901 included the following: THIRD DEGREE - W.A. Arrowood, Guss Ayres, K.W. Bradshaw Sr, R.H. Bradshaw Jr, J.D. Bowman, Jakie Bowman, W.G. Bowman, S.A. Buchanan, Stokes Buchanan, Arthur Buchanan, W.B. Buchanan, M.L. Buchanan, John Buchanan, George L. Buchanan, L.F. Burleson, **W.A. Burleson** (*second row with white sash holding spear – is my guess in the photo*), Marvell Burleson, W.C. Burleson, Len Burleson, Nat Burleson, S.B. Byrd, R.V. Byrd, A.C. Briggs, Wesley Bryant, M. Burris, C.C. Butler, C.C. Boone, W.W. Conley, David Cooke, Flem Cooke, J.J. Conley, W.R. Campbell, J.W. Crawford. W.L. Chaffin, John Cox, N.H. Deyton, Penley Deyton, R.C. Deyton, W.F. Dodson, Robert Ellis, J.E. Ellis, Miller Francis, R.O. Francis, M.L. Gouge, Erwln Gouge, W.M. Gouge, Landon Gouge, Lenard Gouge, D.C. Gage, W.B. Greene, Jessie Greene, David Greene, Chas. E. Greene, Heap Greene, Clapp Greene, Isaac Greene, John D. Gribble, W.T. Garrison, Louis Garland, Monroe Garland, C.C. Garland, Andrew Garland, Wesley Garland, Will Garland, Green Lee Holder, W.F. Hughes, Garrett Hughes, Charles Hughes, Jessie Hoskins, J.H. Hoover, J. E. Henderson, S.G. Hutchins, M.C. Houston, John F. Hampton, S.D. Hampton, J. S. Hoilman, David Hinson, Lee R. Huddleton, Dock Hart, John Jarrett, Henry Lewis, Ervin Lewis, W.L. McNeill, A.R. McNeill, G.D. McNeill. J.L. McKinney, Jonce L. McKinney, T.M. McKinney, John McKinney, Isaac McKinney, Moses McKinney, T.M. McCourry, J.T. McKernah, W.M. Mosley, C.B. Morgan, J.H. Poteat, W.G. Poteat, John Peterson, S.D. Peterson, D.M. Phillips, George K. Pritchard, J.W. Quinn, J.T. Rathbone, Ancil Randolph, C.F. Randolph, F.M. Reed, Welzle Roberson, W.A. Roberson, DR C.E. Smith, John Slagle Sr, John Slagle Jr, Charles Slagle, Will Slagle, John Stewart, Charles Shuffler, James Street, Nathan Street, Calvin Street, J.S. Sparks, D.H. Tappan, Joseph Tipton, J.P. Thomas, D.P. Thomas, S.F. Thomas, M.W. Thomas, Albert Thomas, Rev. J.C. Thomas, T.C. Turby, R.G. Wilson, Johnson Wilson, Albert Wilson, Moses Webb, John Whitson, Don Whitson, J.S. Washburn, W.J. Waycaster, W.M. Woody, Gill Woody, C.R. Yelton, William Yelton, David Yelton. Sam Yelton, J.B. Yelton, M. T. Young, Sam Young, Dr. V.R. Butt.
Photo - Janie Ledford Cook.

taxes were discussed and became the center of conversation. Anderson had reason to believe that Jake Randolph, the land assessor for Little Rock Creek, was recording false information about his taxable assets and was spreading lies about his integrity to others in the community. According to the testimony of Cain Freeman, Randolph had said on an earlier date that Anderson Burleson does not regard his oath. It was gossip that fueled a feud that was destined to culminate in violence.

When Jake Randolph entered the store that humid day, nobody expected that a life would be lost. Upon seeing Jake, Burleson vehemently demanded answers. Not getting any, he reportedly struck Jake in the face. The two then exchanged insults which made both men's tempers flare. After being separated by two store keepers, more insults followed. As Anderson approached Randolph, Jake held an open pocket knife under his shirt. When the two men came together, Randolph pulled the knife from under his shirt and stabbed Burleson in the chest. Knowing that he had hurt Anderson badly, Jake quickly left the store. After being stabbed, Burleson stumbled backwards and collapsed on the floor. He died within five minutes as the store clerk stood in shock. Burleson's brothers next found Randolph riding his horse down a back road that led away from his house. The brothers brought Randolph in at gun point to the sheriff's office in Bakersville. J.D. Burleson, a brother to Anderson, pressed formal charges against Randolph for the murder of his older sibling. The state decided to prosecute Randolph for the charge of first degree murder. In September, Randolph was taken to Marion where his council (Attorneys for J.C. Randolph were W.L. Lambert and Black T. Ragland) waived a preliminary hearing as to the legality of Randolph's imprisonment. Jake was denied bail and ordered to be retained in the Bakersville Jail. The date for the trial was set for November 17, 1907 but was postponed until July of 1908. After a trial that brought statewide attention, Judge R.B. Pebbles said that the State could not prosecute for first degree murder due to the nature of the incident. The judge declared that Randolph acted in self-defense and as a result, did not premeditate to kill Anderson Burleson. The

State, finding that it could not prosecute Randolph on the charge of first degree murder did not take action to pursue any other charges. Maybe because the family did not want to push for more litigation or reasons beyond the scope of the research, Randolph was not tried for manslaughter or second degree murder. Upon the verdict, Jake was exonerated of his charge and eventually moved to Asheville. The following pages contain testimonies from some of the actual court documents. Maybe they will prove insightful in bringing closure to the mystery surrounding the death of my Great-Great-Grandfather Anderson Burleson.

Chapter 5:

More About the Burleson Murder

---

*"NORTH CAROLINA TRAGEDY. **Treasurer Stabs County Commissioner to Death With Pocket Knife. Bakersville, N.C., June 30** – County Treasurer J.C. Randolph stabbed County Commissioner Anderson Burleson to death with a pocket knife near here Thursday. The killing followed a dispute over tax returns. Randolph was afterward badly beaten by brothers of Burleson, one of whom is a state senator."*

-The Salt Lake Herald, Utah (1907)

In order to provide an accurate account of Anderson's death, I have copied the actual documents, testimonies and newspaper articles that were used in the case of the State vs. Jake Randolph. The statements that I have rewritten were found in the Mitchell Courthouse and do not reflect the diction's of the actual trial. The testimonies were taken from a hearing that was held in the Marion Courthouse two months after the incident.

"Upon the oath of J Dosser Burleson, brother to Anderson Burleson, setting forth that J. C. Randolph did on or about the 27th day of June 1907, unlawfully kill and murder one Anderson Burleson, by stabbing him with a knife. A warrant of arrest was issued and delivered on the 27th day of June 1907, to J W Bryant sheriff to be served on the J C Randolph warrant returned on the 27th day of June 1907. Executed by arresting the defendant and producing him in Court, and the following had. The defendant through his counsel comes into Court and waived a preliminary hearing of cause where upon the defendant

is bound over to appear at the November term of Mitchell County Superior Court, to be held on the 16 day of November 1907 for the said County of Mitchell. And the Court being of the opinion it is not a bailable case, the defendant is remanded to jail until otherwise discharged by the Court."
-Mitchell County Court Records (1907)

Jake Randolph's Testimony

"Jake Randolph being sworn says, 'I am the defendant above named, In June this year I went into the store of Burleson Brothers at Glen Ayre in Mitchell County. Anderson, Clingman, and Grant Burleson were present, last two are brothers and next cousin to Anderson.

I was the land assessor for Little Rock Creek Township. Anderson Burleson came upon me, and said don't you want to swear to some more God d___ lies on me in giving in my taxes. He seemed very mad. He kept coming toward me.

I said, 'What do you mean, explain yourself,'

He said, 'God d___ you, I mean just what I said.'

As soon as he got in reach of me, he began to slap me on the face with his open hands, first one side and then the other. I backed from him begging him at the same time not to hit me and that I had been sick and was not able to fight him and did not want to do so. I had nothing against him. Knowing his disposition as I did, I knew if I offered to strike him he would never stop until he killed me. I continued to back until I got out of his reach, he rushed upon me and grabbed my neck and began to beat me with his fist.

I asked Clingman Burleson to take him off of me, that I was sick and not to let him hurt me.

Clingman got him off me. We had by that time got nearly to the rear-end of the store. Anderson Burleson then cursed me and called me a God d___ son of a bitch and all kinds of bad names. I said, 'Anderson

This 1899 two-dollar silver certificate was said to have been in Anderson's wallet on the day he was killed. Photo - Allen Cook.

call me what you please but for the sake of my good mothers name, don't call me a son of a bitch.'

When at near end of counter, Anderson came towards me still cursing and accusing me of using brutality. And I said, 'What did you do 4 years ago?'

He was then 8 or 10 feet from me and had made a kind of halt. When I said this, he made for me, saying, 'God d___ it, I will mash you.' He grabbed me by the shoulder with his right hand, he was left-handed. I could not get to the door, I backed towards the counter and came into contact with some boxes, when he struck me in the mouth with his left hand and knocked me up against the counter.

Up to this time I had made no attempt to strike him. He ran his left hand into his pocket like he was trying to get something. I did not know whether it was a knife or what. I thought he was going to kill me. I got out my knife and by the time I got it opened he struck me on the head. This blow rendered me unconscious and the next thing I remembered, I was standing upon my feet. He had let me loose and was walking backwards.

Thinking he was going to get something to hit me with, I started to run, not knowing I had cut him. I ran out of the store, fearing he was going to hit me, and looked back to see if he was coming or going to come at me, and I saw him sinking down, and I knew then that I had

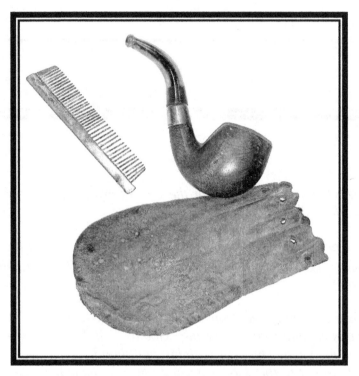

Photo of Anderson Burleson's briar wood tobacco pipe, pouch and beard comb. Photo - Allen Cook.

badly hurt him.

I told Mrs. Bowman that I was afraid I had hurt Mr. Burleson and to go in the store and see if she could do anything for him.

I got on horse and went home and put on clean clothes and started to Bakersville to give myself up. I met two of Anderson's brothers, they commanded me to throw up my hands. I did so and they carried me to Bakersville. I was not on the regular road to Bakersville, but on the above way, I did not go regular road because I was afraid I would meet up with Anderson's brothers. My health has been bad for 9 years, but little use of right arm for 12 months.

Anderson Burleson was a man of big frame and a stout man. "

Cross examined

"Store had one door about 40 feet long and 25 feet wide.

Anderson Burleson, Clingman Burleson, Grant Burleson a 12 or 13 year old boy was there when I went in. Do not know when he left.

Never had any trouble with Anderson before, lived 1/2 mile of him, never heard of his killing anyone. I heard he had beaten one of his cousins nearly to death in Bakersville. I heard of his throwing a rock on Tom Edwards, his gun on two of the Biddix boys. I knew of his being indicted once, he was acquitted.

I did not try to ward off the blows.

Clingman and Grant were cousins to Anderson, I never advanced towards Anderson. I remember getting out my knife and opening it with both hands. When I came to myself I found my knife in my hands and Anderson was bleeding from the left breast. I don't know how many times I cut him.

I was indicted for carrying a concealed weapon, acquitted. I was also indicted for trespass. I once cut a place in the shin of West English. I drew knife on my son-in-law, he had a pistol drawn on me.

Anderson died from cut I gave him, he lived about 5 minutes.

Sworn to and subscribed before me this Sept 17, 1907, JC Randolph. "
-Mitchell County Court Records (1907)

Wylie Clingman Burleson's Testimony

Wylie Clingman Burleson was the store keeper of Burleson Brothers Grocery. His son, Fate Burleson owned the store and later sold it to Ford Greene where it was passed through the generations to the current owner, Dwight Thomas. Wylie Clingman was a first cousin to Anderson Burleson and an eye witness to the stabbing. Anderson also had a brother named Clingman, so when reading the account do not confuse the names. Wylie Clingman was called as witness for the state. His testimony is as follows:

"Clingman Burleson being duly sworn says; 'I am first cousin to Anderson Burleson, Anderson was sitting on counter or bench, Randolph came in. Burleson got up and went towards him and said, 'Jake, I reckon you want to swear to some more God d___ lies-'

Jake says, 'What do you mean,' Jake is the commissioner.

Anderson said, 'I mean just what I said,' and drew back like he was going to hit Jake.

Jake said, 'Don't hit me, I am not able fight you.' Several words passed which I do not recollect, Jake went towards the other end of store and Anderson followed him and slapped him twice in the face on each side. I got over to where they were as quick as I could. I pushed Jake towards one end of store and my brother Grant pushed Anderson towards the other end. I told them to quit. They kept jimmying back at each other.

Jake run his hand in his pocket, then Anderson saw his hand in his pocket and said, 'Don't make a move, I will mash you in and mash you all to pieces.' I pushed Randolph to the end of the counter and thought the difficulty was over with and walked behind the counter.

Burleson said to Jake, 'You are nothing but a low down son of a bitch.'

Jake said, 'Anderson, don't call me that. I have too good a mother to be called a son of a bitch.'

Anderson said, 'You burnt your barn for the insurance, you killed your old uncles cattle.'

Jake pointed at Anderson and said, 'You will dearly pay for this,'

Anderson said, 'Damn you, I can do it.'

They spoke some other words, which I do not remember.

Jake said, 'You know what you did 4 years ago!'

Anderson said, 'Don't you say that again,' and started towards Jake.

I saw them run together. Anderson looked like he struck Jake in the face and Jake looked like he struck Anderson under his left arm. When I saw them going together I ran from around the counter.

By the time I got to the end of the counter, Randolph staggered out of the door. Anderson turned and looked after Jake and said something to me which I did not understand. I spoke to Anderson and he did not answer. I took hold of him, he fell back and died in a few minutes.

He was cut under the left arm, under the left nipple, and his left hand was cut and clothes across his stomach were cut.

Between the time Anderson slapped Jake and the cutting took place about one or two minutes elapsed."

Cross examined.

"When Randolph started towards Anderson he went in a fast walk. At this time the door was opened behind him and the cutting took place immediately after they went together, something like 1/4 of minute. I never saw anything in Anderson's hand. I never saw Randolph's' knife either."
-Mitchell County Court Records (1907)

Cain Freeman's Testimony
This testimony for the state was struck out due to a technicality.

"Cain Freeman being duly sworn says defendant, I, and Ellick Buchanan were appointed list workers and assessors. On first morning in June, Randolph said let us go into this regardless of friends. He said I don't want it like it was four years ago. He said Anderson Burleson does not regard his oath."
-Mitchell County Court Records (1907)

The Impact on the Community
The impending case of the State vs. Jake Randolph served to cause differing opinions among members of the Glen Ayre Community. Both Anderson and Jake were major players in the political climate of the time. Both men previously held the office of county commissioner and had worked as tax assessors four years earlier. Competition between the two men may have led to mudslinging which severely got out of hand on that hot late June afternoon. Newspapers around the state and country reported the tragedy.

TRAGEDY IN MITCHELL.
Former County Treasurer Cuts Former Commissioner Burleson To Death With a Pocket Knife – Randolph Is Later Attacked by Burleson's Brothers, But Finally Surrenders to the Authorities.
BAKERSVILLE, June 30 – J.C. Randolph killed Anderson Burleson at Glen Ayre Thursday afternoon. Mr. Randolph was tax-lister and Mr. Burleson accused him of listing his property too high. Burleson slapped Randolph a time or two with his open hand and then struck him on the side of the head with his fist. Mr. Randolph drew a pocket knife and cut Burleson three or four times, killing him instantly.

Randolph went to his home, put on other clothes and started to Bakersville to give up to the authorities, when he was met by some of Burleson's brothers, who beat him badly, but a young man or two who happened to be at hand, put a stop to that part of the business.

Both of these men stood high in the community. Mr. Randolph has been treasurer of the county and Mr. Burleson a county commissioner.

I visited Mr. Randolph in jail this morning and found him able to talk. He deplores the affair very much. Both men have large and excellent families.

Burleson was a brother of State Senator Burleson.
-Western Sentinel, North Carolina (1907)

TAX QUARREL WAS FATAL.
North Carolina Farmer Stabbed to Death by Assessor.
Special to The Washington Post.
Bristol, Tenn, June 29, - A dispatch from Bakersville, N.C. says that Anderson Burleson, a prominent farmer of that place, was stabbed to death by Tax Assessor J.K. Randolph there this afternoon. The trouble grew out of the assessment of Burleson's property. The two men met near the passenger depot at Bakersville late this afternoon. Burleson charged that Randolph had assessed his property at double its proper assessment and the fight followed. The tax assessor stabbed Burleson just above the heart and he died instantly.

Randolph was arrested and will be given a preliminary hearing Monday.
-The Washington Post, Washington D.C. (1907)

With a toxic mix of politics and family loyalties, supporters and friends of Anderson sympathized with the Burleson family while those who backed Jake Randolph pleaded for his freedom. Below are some of the character witnesses that appeared for Randolph and the State:

"Subpoenas were issued to A.W. Buchanan to appear on the part of the defendant J.C. Randolph to appear the 17 day of Sept. before judge R.B. Peebles.

Subpoenas were issued to appear at the Nov 1907 term in Superior Court to W.C. Burleson, Grant Burleson, Cain Freeman and Eb Greene on the part of the State; those subpoenaed for the defendant were G.W. Greene, H.B. Buchanan, D.C. Hopson, John McKinney, Fred Gouge, Wm. Ellis, T.C. Edwards, Yates Biddix, John Biddix, Mrs. Anna Bowman, Jess Miller, A.W. Buchanan, Burk Woody, Jake Bowman, Joe Greene, Waits Burleson, V.R. Butt, Herby Gouge; others as to appear, although it is not indicated on what part were Sanders Edwards, C.W. McKinney, Stokes Buchanan, Tilman McKinney, H.G. Woody.

Subpoenas issued for special term in Superior Court for July 1908 on the part of the defendant included Will Ellis, Fred Gouge, John McKinney, A.W. Buchanan, H.B. Buchanan, Mrs. Anna Bowman, Milt Holder, Cleo Hopson, Jess Miller, G.W. Green, Aswell Childers, Oscar Bowman, Burnie Green, T.C. Edwards P.W. Slage, Cleveland Ayers, M.F. Young, W.K. Buchanan, C.A. Young, Ed Young, Henry Canipe, S.D. Tipton, Henry Rathbone, Isaac McIntuff, Sanders Edwards, Joe Green, C.W. McKinney, J.C. Bowman, Wates Burleson, John Hopson, Sr., I.H. Bailey, W.B. Bowman, Rev. S.M. Greene, J.S. Potear, W.G. Poteat, W.J. Slage, M.B. Wilson, D.M. Cook, R.J. Young, E.B. Greene, on part of State included John Houston, Burnie Greene, George Gouge, Will Ellis, Russ Buchanan, Sam McKinney, John Hopson, W.C. Burleson, Grant Burleson, Cain Freeman, Harrison Hughes, G.B. Ledford, J.M. Ayers, Wm Greene, Saw Burleson, J.A. Buchanan.

During this term of Superior Court, July 8, The jurors for the state upon their oaths present, that Jacob C Randolph, late of the County of Mitchell, on the 27th day of June 1907, with force and arms, at and in the county a foresaw, feloniously willfully and of his malice aforethought, did kill and murder Anderson Burleson, contrary to the form of the state in such cases made and provided, and against the peace and dignity of the state. D.H. Hughes foreman of the Grand Jury.

A request for bail was made in the amount of 5000.00, and the following signed the bond, 1000.00 C.A. Wise, F.P. Slagle, J.L. Bowman, R.B. McKinney, 2000.00 Nat Blevins.

Subpoenas issued in Superior Court for Nov. 16, 1908 on the part of the defendant include, Elic English, Henry Rathbone Jr., John Hopson Sr., Saunders Edwards, J.C. Ayers, John Randolph, Rich Randolph, W.K. Buchanan, S.M. Greene, R.J. Young, I.H. Bailey, Dr. V.R. Butts, M.C. Wilson, Wiley Gouge, C.E. Young, W.M. Ellis, Fred Gouge, E.B. Greene, Ed Young, Henry Kanipe, A.W. Buchanan, Jesse Miller, Cole Hopson, Bernie Greene, H.B. Buchanan, Waits Burleson, Joe Greene, Charley Renfro, Charley McInturff, Stokes Buchanan, Jim Byrd, Isaac McKinney, Lafayette McKinney, Aaron Ellis, L. F. Burleson; on part of the state include W.C. Burleson, Grant Burleson, Cain Freeman, George Gouge, Will Ellis, Rus Buchanan, Sam McKinney, John Hobson, Steve Miller, Windell Slagle and Grover Greene, Rubin Ledford, Sherriff Bryant, Lafayette McKinney, Dr. Bradhaw, Marion Ayers, J.M. Ledford, Dosser Burleson, Nex McKinney, N.W. Byrd."
-Mitchell County Court Records *(1907)*

With a full courtroom, the trial of Jake Randolph was the first high profile murder case in the new Bakersville Courthouse. The state assigned Colonel R.Z. Linney to prosecute Randolph. Linney was known as an eloquent and powerful speaker. During the closing argument of the State vs. Jake Randolph, Linney delivered a masterful and dramatic closing speech. The scene was reported in newspapers throughout the state.

MR. LINNEY COLLAPSED.
Became Exhausted While Making the Closing Argument in a Murder Case in Mitchell Superior Court.
Mr. Locke Craig tells the Asheville Citizen of a dramatic incident in Mitchell County Superior Court at Bakersville last week, while Hon. R.Z. Linney, of Taylorsville, was making the closing argument in a murder trial. Jacob Randolph was the defendant and acquitted. Mr.

Linney appeared for the prosecution and Mr. Craig's account of his speech is thus quoted by the Citizen:

"The dramatic scenes in the argument of Colonel R.Z. Linney, who made the closing speech in the case, will long be remembered by all the people of that section. Colonel Linney has for many years been conspicuous in North Carolina, noted for his eloquence and power, but I think on this occasion he surpassed himself. He spoke on Monday night, after supper. The court house was packed with people. It was dimly lighted except in the bar. The packed crowd heard with breathless interest and tense stillness the utterances of the great orator. He was certainly masterful in his eloquence. I have never heard it surpassed. At times he spoke in suppressed tones; at times his voice was like a trumpet, and his face was illumined by his thought.

It so happened that the defendant sat immediately under him in the bright light. He was not guilty and he knew it, and he showed it in his clear cut, handsome face, as he listened to the powerful advocate who thundered against him. Colonel Linney spoke for more than an hour, and then the collapse came – before he reached the conclusion of his speech – he sank down in a chair, exhausted. The judge adjourned court and for several hours it was feared that Colonel Linney would not rally, but about half past two o'clock he did, and will undoubtedly recover. In his speech, among other things, he talked of life and death and eternity in a way that would give renown to the greatest preacher. Those who heard him will bear me out in my praise of him. When a man does a great thing I think he ought to have credit for it before he dies."

-*The News-Herald,* North Carolina (1908)

After the trial, the brothers of Anderson reportedly threatened Randolph. Jake began to fear for his life. As a result, a restraining order was taken out against the Burlesons. Shortly after the trial, Jake Randolph and his family moved to Asheville.

The bitterness in the community slowly subsided and the Burlesons began, once again, to climb the political ladder. In the years to come, Lafayette Burleson, a first cousin to Anderson Burleson, was elected to the position of Mitchell County sheriff and Anderson's youngest son, Jeter Burleson became a well-known public servant which included the offices of Clerk of Superior Court and North Carolina State Representative. Today, descendants of both families have laid the past to rest. The community has rebounded from that infamous killing and the relatives of the Randolphs and Burlesons have even married into each other.

Chapter 6:
Roan Valley Revenge

"Good banjo picker and fiddler. Had in his possession when last seen a 30 calibre German Luger revolver, with which he did the shooting."

-Mack Edwards Wanted Poster, North Carolina *(1922)*

On a hot August afternoon, James Edwards and his mule, Maude, ambled along an old cow trail across his neighbor's property. James had brought ears of corn and some early apples to his son, Mack, who was working on a logging crew in Roan Valley. The shortcut that James and Maude were using cut out considerable time and would enable him to get home in time for supper. The frail old mountain man felt too tired and hot to take the long way home. Knowing the land was owned by Gilbert Woody, James figured that Gilbert would probably not care if he used the trail this one time. At worst, he thought that he might be sternly warned against trespassing and then be allowed to pass on over to his house and still get supper with time to spare. As James slipped across the Woody property, Mr. Woody's sons sighted the elderly man as he cut across an open field. Expecting to be told to leave, James waited as the three riders approached. The events that followed led to the culmination of hard feelings and ended in bloodshed.

Chunks of grass and dirt flew out from the hooves of the galloping horses as Gilbert Woody's two sons, Burke and Bascomb, pulled the reins on their steeds. In the rear was one of Mr. Woody's hired hands who helped move the grazing sheep from pasture to pasture in the summer months. The three riders halted their horses in front of James as Bascomb Woody began to dismount his sorrel Tennessee Walking

75

Horse. Mr. Edwards greeted the boys with a friendly natured "Howdy." The Woody's responded by asking, "Why are you on our land." James then told his story on how it was quicker and easier to pass across the fields to his house and that he was trying to get home in time for supper. He apologized for being on the property, but that did not seem to suffice for Burke and Bascomb Woody. Without a warning, the two boys pulled the old man off of the mule and kicked him in the gut. They said that trespassers need to be taught a lesson and scattered all the provisions that he was hauling on his mule along the trail. Bruised and beaten, James Edwards watched as the three riders saddled up. As Bascomb Woody turned his horse to go home he shouted, "If I see you again, I'll shoot your sorry ass." James Edwards dusted the dirt off his britches, caught Maude, and slowly crossed over to his cabin. Because James figured that he may have been beaten justifiably for trespassing, and no real harm was done, he decided to let the matter rest and tell nobody.

The next day Mack Edwards, James's son, was at J.M. Ayers store in Roan Valley and heard what happened to his father from neighbors Fate Holder and Ben Riddle. They claimed to have seen the incident while working in a bordering field. As Fate and Ben described to Mack the details of what they had seen, the Edwards boy felt his anger begin to rise. Mack Edwards had been home from World War I military service for about a year and a half. Young Mack had grown up with Burke and Bascomb and did not figure they would beat up an elderly man. Not knowing whether or not the rumor he had heard was true, Mack decided to visit Gilbert Woody and see for himself. It made Mack mad to think that some boys his age would pick on his father and he figured on a fight if the story Ben and Fate had told was true. Mack went back home to confront his father but he had went to Glen Ayre on business. Mack's sister said that he had been in a scrap but did not want to make an issue of the incident. Upon hearing his sister's plea, Mack went to his closet and pulled up a floor board to uncover the German Luger pistol that he had pulled off a dead soldier three and a half years earlier. As the cold steel contrasted the hot August heat on Mack's hands, times in France flashed through his mind. Visions of death and destruction caused a normal conscious to turn to animal like instinct. Mack put six bullets in the pistol and stuck it in his pants where the brown flannel shirt that he wore would fall over it. If the boys tried to start anything, young Mack decided the gun would even the odds. Mack figured to talk to Gilbert and see why his boys had beat up an elderly man like his father. He also decided that he would serve notice on the Woody's. If they ever ganged up on anyone in his family again, the Woody's would regret it.

Mack walked up to the fence surrounding Gilbert Woody's house and saw Burke standing by the barn. Mack asked Burke about the beating and demanded an explanation. Burke apologized and said that it wouldn't happen again. Satisfied, Mack turned to walk away. As he started down the road that led away from the Woody cabin, he heard a door slam and looked over his shoulder to see Gilbert standing on the porch with a leather strap. The strap was usually used at the sawmill for latching logs to wagons, but today Mack figured the strap would be put to a different use. Gilbert started down the steps in a fast walk towards Mack Edwards and said that if he had anything to say, to say it to him. Bascomb also came out of the house following his father. Burke walked out of the barn to see what was going on. When he saw that his dad and brother were walking towards Mack, he picked up the branding iron which was conveniently leaned against the barn door. Gilbert started cursing Mack and told him that he had better start running. Mack stood his ground.

When Mack saw Gilbert charging towards him wildly swinging the leather strap, instincts that had not been realized since France came into play. With a quick draw, young Mack grasped the German Luger pistol from beneath his shirt. Looking down the barrel, Mack saw the anger in Gilbert's face turn frantic...and then expressionless. Upon seeing his father fall to the ground, Bascomb Woody charged towards Mack Edwards in a wild run. Edwards quickly brought the pistol to a point just below Bascomb's nose and squeezed the trigger. Shocked and scared, Burke took cover beside the house. He tried to reach for a pistol on the porch but Mack shot him in the hand. The whole scene lasted less than a minute. When Mack saw that all the threats were gone, he was gripped by fear from the drastic actions that he had taken. He knew that the shots would draw half the community and decided that he would make a run across the nearby ridge for the settlement of Roaring Creek.

As Mack ran for the woods, Burke crawled towards his dying father. The bullet had hit Gilbert in the face and he knew that his Daddy was not going to last long. Looking down on Bascomb, Burke saw that life had instantly departed from his brother. Enraged and hurt, Burke quickly wrapped his bloody hand with an old rag in the barn and went inside the house to get the rifle. Burke then ran into the woods in pursuit of Mack. It was not long before Mack's trail grew cold. Injured and mad, Burke turned back to get help for his father and assemble a posse to capture Mack Edwards. The sheriff and his deputies used blood hounds to pursue Mack to the Little Yellow Pass. Once in the backwoods, they were hesitant to pursue the gunman further because the land was steep and they were afraid Edwards would bushwhack the posse in one of the Rocky passes.

Wanted posters like the one to the right were circulated throughout the state in hopes that Mack Edwards would be captured. The "Description" section of the poster reads as follows:
Description
Age 28 – looks younger. About 5 feet 7 inches tall. Weight about 135 pounds. Light, sandy hair, slightly bald. Square shoulders, pitched slightly forward. Each little finger crooked a little. Blue eyes, with a rather wild expression and a peculiar movement of the eyes which is very noticeable. Red face, straight nose and face generally square. Forehead slopes back a little. Has rather small hands and little freckled on face and hands. Has gentle step and quick motioned. Has had one leg broken just above the ankle, and has slight limp, but hardly noticeable. Wears No. 5 shoes. Good banjo picker and fiddler. Had in his possession when last seen a 30 calibre German Luger revolver, with which he did the shooting. This 19th day of Aug. 1922. Send all communications to R.C. Forbes, Sheriff, Bakersville, N.C. or to Wilson & Lambert Attys, Bakersville, or to NB Woody, Route 1, Bakersville N.C.

REWARD OF $1,500.00

Is Hereby Offered for Apprehension and Delivery of one MACK EDWARDS,

To the Sheriff of Mitchell County, North Carolina.

Who is wanted in Mitchell County, N. C., for shooting and killing H. G. Woody and Bascomb Woody, and seriously wounding N. B. Woody on 5th day of August, 1922, at their home

$400.00 is offered by the State of North Carolina

Under a proclamation of the Governor, Cameron Morrison, dated August 18th, 1922. And

$1,100.00 is by the widow of H. G. Woody, and Son

N. B. WOODY, and is deposited in Merchants & Farmers Bank at Bakersville, and will be paid to the party or parties, entitled to receive the reward.

Description

Age 29, looks younger.
About 5 feet 7 inches tall.
Weight about 135 pounds.
Light sandy hair, slightly bald.
Square shoulders, pitched slightly forward.
Each little finger crooked a little.
Blue eyes, with rather a wild expression and a peculiar movement of the eyes which is very noticeable. Red face, straight nose and face generally square.
Forehead slopes back a little. Has rather small hands and little freckled on face and hands. Has a active step and quick motioned. Has had one leg broken just above the ankle, and has a slight limp, but hardly noticeable. Wears No. 5 shoes. Good banjo picker and fiddler. Had in his possession when last seen, a 30 calibre German Luger revolver, with which he did the shooting.
This 19th day of Aug. 1922.
Send all communications to R. C. Forbes, Sheriff, Bakersville, N. C. or to Wilson & Lambert, Attys, Bakersville, or to N. B. Woody, Route 1, Bakersville, N. C.

reached his oldest sisters house in Roaring Creek where he stocked up on ammunition and food. He then ran for the train depot in the nearby mining town of Cranberry where, the same day, Edwards caught a train that was heading into Tennessee. Not many people knew what became of Mack Edwards after he disappeared. The sheriff issued a reward for his capture, but no one ever caught the young fugitive outlaw. Many of Mack's friends said that he probably moved to Oregon where he had worked in years past as a logger. It was rumored that he would visit his relatives in secret, but the old timers who knew would only grin and say that Mack never came back.

Chapter 7:

More About Roan Valley Revenge

"ALLEGED DESPERADO STILL AT LIBERTY
BAKERSVILLE, AUGUST 8:
Mack Edwards, alleged slayer of H.G. Woody, who
was shot and killed on Little Rock creek in Mitchell
County, Friday, at the same time his two sons,
Bascombe and Burt Woody, were seriously
wounded, is still at liberty. Neither of the boys is
expected to live.

Edwards has the reputation of being a desperate
man. During the late war he evaded until near the
close of the war, when he volunteered and served
about two months at the United States lumber camp
at Vancouver, Wash. The Woody family is very well
to do and highly respected."

-The Charlotte Observer, **North Carolina** *(1921)*

The Woody shooting was one of the most notorious killings on Roan Mountain. As a result, I have provided supplemental research which will add more insight about the event.

The Victims
Gilbert Woody owned a saw mill in Roan Valley which employed his two sons, Bascomb and Burke. Located on the head of Little Rock Creek, Burke Woody owned the property where the shooting took place. The Edwards's owned land along the Northern border of the Woody's property. The Woody land was situated near a valley that made for easy access into Glen Ayre from the Roan. There is some

question, however, as to whether or not the Woody's owned the land where James Edwards was beat up. Some old timers say James was near the saw mill and the boys harassed him on land that they had leased from Cain Freeman.

Upon marrying Fanny Saylor from Washington County, Tennessee, Mr. Woody acquired land in Little Rock Creek to set up a saw milling operation. Gilbert had five children named Molly, Burke, Ida, Laura, and Bascomb. Upon his death, Gilbert owned 14 tracts of land which amounted to about 400 acres. When Mack was not arrested, the Woody family litigated for restitution from the Edwards family. As a result, they acquired foreclosure rights on the properties owned by Mack Edwards.

The Accused
James Edwards was a farmer that lived in Roan Valley. His wife was deceased and I have no record of her name. James' children were Lumen, Mandy, Mary, Saunders, Jacob, and Mack. When neighbors had brought the Woody incident to Mack's attention, the short tempered, youngest son wanted to know why his father had been hurt.

It is not clear as to whether or not Mack went overseas to serve in World War 1 or contracted himself out as a government lumber worker in the Western states. An old timer related to Mack reminisced how Mack had worked out west where he became a sharp shooter. Beyond word of mouth, there is little written facts about Mack's background. My great Uncle, Fiddling Steve Ledford, said that Mack taught him how to play the fiddle. The Wanted Poster also stated that Mack was a good banjo and fiddle player. Mack Edwards was just 29 years old when he began his life as a fugitive. His gun was reported to be a .30 caliber German Luger pistol. Both of the lethal shots that were fired hit the Woody's in an area just below the nose. Newspapers confirmed details of the shooting.

Mountaineers Near Asheville Shoot, Kill and Wound
BY ASSOCIATED PRESS

Asheville, N.C. Aug. 6. – Grady Peterson is dead and A.C. Letterman is in jail at Burnsville, charged with the killing. Letterman is wounded but not seriously and he surrendered to the Yancey County sheriff today. Circumstances leading up to the killing could not be learned as it occurred in a remote section of the mountains.

Used Copper Bullets.

Asheville, N.C. Aug. 6. – Gill Woody was instantly killed, Bert Woody, his son, shot in the mouth and leg. Bass Woody, another son, wounded in the neck by Mack Edwards, it is charged by county authorities, near Bakersville yesterday, according to reports reaching the sheriff here.

Bloodhounds have been placed on the trail of Edwards and a thousand dollar reward has been offered. Cause of the shooting is unknown. Reports are to the effect that the weapon used was a German Luger using copper bullets.

-The Index-Journal, South Carolina (Watson, 1921)

Edward's had a sister who lived in Roaring Creek and it was said that Mack stopped by her house shortly after the shooting. It was speculated by the old timers that she hid her brother from authorities and helped transport him out of the area. Lawmen would often try to catch Edwards as he would slip into the Glen Ayre Community to visit his siblings and play music with the Ledfords at the end of Charles Creek Road. Mack was never caught and likely started a new life under a different name. An article from the Asheville Citizen stated that Mack was arrested in Clintwood Virginia but the arrest turned out to be mistaken identity.

MACK EDWARDS ARRESTED IN CLINTWOOD, VIRGINIA
Is Wanted in Mitchell in Connection With Double Murder There.

BAKERSVILLE, Oct. 5. – A telegram was received by Sheriff Pritchard late yesterday evening that the authorities at Clintwood, Va., have arrested Mack Edwards and placed him in jail. It was reported that Edwards some time ago had a difficulty with Gil Woody, Bas Woody, and Burke Woody near Glen Ayre in Mitchell County, and that Gil Woody and Bass Woody were killed and Burke badly

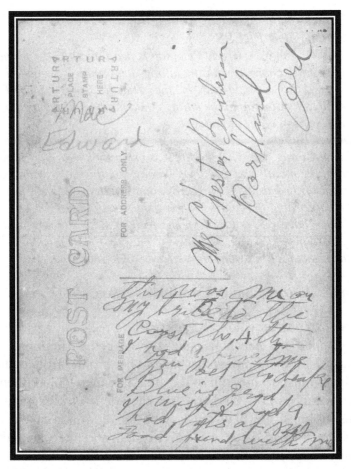

Mack sent letters to his friends and relatives. The photo post card (back left page and front right page) was sent in an envelope to Chester Burleson from Mack when he was on the west coast. Best I can tell, it reads as follows: "This was me on my trip to the coast the 4th. I had a fine time. You bet the dealer. Blue is good. Wish I had 9. I had lots of my good friends with me." It is unknown as to whether this was sent before or after the shooting. Photo – Janie Ledford Cook.

wounded. The report that Edwards was in Clintwood Jail could not be confirmed at a late hour tonight.
*-Asheville Citizen-Times, **North Carolina** (Robinson, 1921)*

Nobody knows what became of Mack Edwards. Mack may have joined relatives who lived in Oregon. Some say he married a Navajo Indian and had a ranch in Wyoming. Allegedly after his wife died, it was said that Mack would occasionally return to Roaring Creek to visit his sister. In his old age, one story goes that Mack died in a train accident while living with his sister in Marion.

Mack Edwards was remembered as an old-time banjo picker, fiddle player and dancer. My Great Uncle, Fiddling Steve Ledford credited Mack with teaching him to play the fiddle. The story goes that when

Steve was seven years old, Mack taught him the tune "Whistling Rufus." Steve eventually went on to play his fiddle on the stage of the Grand Old Opry in Nashville, Tennessee. Subsequently, Steve Ledford married Mack's cousin Stella Mae Edwards.

Old Timer Recollections

My Grandpa Charlie Ledford, Cleo and Edna Edwards, and Tommy Lee Edwards would recount the Mac Edwards story to me when I was just a boy living in Glen Ayre. The following recollections are my memories from those old timers who have passed on since the original printing of this book in 1997. The following account is a general consensus of what I was told by them.

The story went that James Edwards and his mule cut through a gap near Round Mountain in route to his adjoining property. Gilbert Woody (who went by Gil) owned the property where the shortcut was located. I can remember Cleo Edwards pointing towards the fields above Old Roan Mountain Road when he described the location of the Woody property. One day as James Edwards was crossing the gap, Gil Woody's sons, Lumen Bascomb (Bass) and Burke, pulled the elderly man off his mule, beat him with a leather strap, and warned him not to trespass over their land. Local farmhands, Fate Holder and a man by the last name of Riddle witnessed the incident and told James' son, Mack.

The next day, Mack Edwards paid a visit to the home of Gilbert Woody to ask questions about the harsh treatment of his father. According to the old timers, Burke told Mack that it had been settled and would not happen again. Mack started to walk away when Bass Woody and Gil Woody stepped out of the nearby barn. Gil was said to have been holding a long leather belt which was used to strap lumber and logs to wagons. Whether the same strap had been used on Mack's father "to teach him a lesson" is not known. Unlike Burke, Bass and Gil confronted Mack and warned him that he would receive the same beating that was given to his father if he was ever caught on the property. Feeling outnumbered and threatened by the strap in

Gil's hand, Mack drew his .30 caliber German Luger. With four quick shots he killed Gil and Bass. Burke was wounded in the hand and neck. It was said by my father-in-law, Joe Garland, that his father, Arthur Garland had heard that Mack had done the shooting all while on horseback which, if true, would certainly confirm his reputation as being a sharp shooter. Lumen Bascomb Woody was killed on August 10, 1921. His father Gilbert Woody died five days later.

The old timers told me the escape route that Edwards took after the shooting. Armed and dangerous, Mack passed near present day Roan Valley Baptist Church and skirted up and around the base of Chimney Ridge. He was said to have followed the Bee Tree Ridgeline up to the Grassy Ridge where he then crossed into Roaring Creek in Avery County. Cleo Edwards told me how the sheriff used bloodhounds to track Mack. As the track progressed into the rocky bluffs near Grassy Ridge, the sheriff called the trackers back for fear that they would be ambushed. It was said that Mack had a sister by the name of Mary in Roaring Creek who gave him food and money to catch a train. Mack was never arrested. After the shooting, it was said that Edwards secretly visited Glen Ayre to see family and friends on rare occasions.

Chapter 8:

Roan Mountain Dew

"February 14, 1895 - Western North Carolina is strictly temperate now. The moonshine liquor is frozen."

−The Comet, **Tennessee (1895)**

Some broken jars and a few fire blackened rocks are all that remains at the illegal distillery site of my Great Grandpa, Anderson "Waites" Ledford. The still was located in what was termed by mountain folks as "a deep, lonesome holler where the sun don't never shine." But the moon did shine at Waites Ledford's still. Situated in the shadow of Roan Mountain, the still produced many a jug of Roan Mountain Dew for the friends and neighbors of Waites during the early days of prohibition. Hidden beneath the Laurel Ridge near a springhead in the backwoods of the Charles Creek, Ledford and his family manufactured their brew in notorious Mitchell County - home of the perfect moonshine still!

If one were to have walked up on A.W. Ledford's mountain still, they would have seen a fire pit, a large mash pot with a copper hood, and two wooden barrels all connected together with pipes and copper tubing. In addition, mason jars, sacks of sugar and barrels of fermenting corn mash were usually scattered around the Ledford moonshine still. Situated on the side of Laurel Ridge, Waites' sons had an elevated vantage point where they could easily watch the road

The typical moonshine still consists of a cooker with a removable top called a "horsehead." The coiled pipe is called the "worm" or condenser. Antique Still Courtesy of Joe Garland.

for unwanted visitors. As a result, the A.W. Ledford still produced many a jug of Roan Mountain Dew while in operation.

The distillery of Waites Ledford followed a design that had been passed down through the generations. Typical of an early 1900s backwoods distillery, the Ledford site consisted of a rock fire pit, a mash pot and two oak barrels, all constructed adjacent to a cool flowing mountain spring. The rock enclosure served to keep an even temperature during the cooking process and provided a base for the cooking section of the distillery. Most illegal whiskey makers preferred oak firewood to cook the mash since seasoned oak does not let off much smoke that would alert revenuers of the still's location. A large, copper mash pot was placed over the hot oak coals. Ledford and his sons would carefully heat a pot of "corn mash" to 170 degrees - enough heat to evaporate the alcohol but not boil the water. Attached and sealed by an oatmeal paste to the top of the corn mash cooking pot was a smoke stack looking contraption referred to by old timers as the "horse head" or "cap." The horse head directed the alcoholic steam from the cooking mash into an oak barrel called the "thump keg." Steam would then pass through the barrel and make a thumping sound, thus the name thump keg. The thump keg was often partially filled with fermented apples, blackberries or peaches to impart a custom flavor to the steam. The final step in the distillation process was condensing the gaseous alcohol into liquid form. This was accomplished by a tightly coiled copper tube known by backwoods shiners as the "worm." The worm directed Ledford's intoxicating vapor from the thump keg into a second oak barrel (filled with cold Roan Mountain spring water) called the "flakestand." The flakestand served to cool the worm and condense the alcoholic steam into liquid form. The sweet spirits exited the worm and dripped into the catch can - finally ending up in mason jars and clay jugs.

For many mountain families, making moonshine was a matter of tradition. The typical family recipe involved fermenting a mix of sugar, corn, yeast and water in a large barrel or tub. The brew would "work" for four to six days as the yeast turned the corn and sugar into a beer like mixture. A good whiskey maker always took the time to prepare a properly fermented beer (also called mash) to boil in his still. Most old-time moonshiners will attest that the taste of a batch of Roan Mountain Dew is directly related to the quality of the mash.

In the *Shadow* of the
ROAN

An article from the Charlotte Observer in 1876 tales the story of a peculiar mix of mash:

"STATE NEWS....John Tipton is a blockade runner in Mitchell County, and had a dog which he valued very much. The dog, however, turned up missing, a few weeks ago, and John missed him very much, but nevertheless he kept at work with his still tubs, when one day as he was stirring up the mash, he felt something in the bottom of the tub and his curiosity being excited he succeeded in bringing to the surface of the still tub his missing dog in a state of partial decomposition. John had made one or two runs out of the tub after the dog was missed so he concluded to finish the remainder. The dog, in trying to lap some of the beer out of the tub, had fallen in and become one of the component parts of that and previous runs of whiskey. John D. said that he thought that 'ar licker had a sorter quar taste, but he did not know what was the matter until he fished up the dog, hair and all. The Bakersville Republican fathers this yarn."
-Charlotte Observer, **North Carolina** (1876)

"Cook'n off a batch" was often done at night. Illicit whiskey earned the name "moonshine" because it was distilled beneath the light of the moon in order to escape the notice of revenuers. Making a run of Roan Mountain Dew under the cover of darkness was an age-old tradition passed along through many generations and a rite only afforded to those who could be trusted. The evening air around an active still was often filled with the smell of oak smoke, fermented corn and oatmeal. Many times, as in the case of the Ledford still, friends and family would bring musical instruments and pick traditional tunes while the brew cooked. The beat of alcoholic steam bubbling through the thump keg often kept time with a clanking banjo, twanging guitar and crying fiddle. A rural still was often a festive place to be at night – unless you were an outsider or revenuer.

Moonshine stills like the one in the above photograph were used to make Roan Mountain Dew. The mash pot is pictured left, the thump keg is the middle portion and the condenser, also called the "worm" is to the right. The end barrel which holds the worm is referred to as the "flakestand." Antique Still Courtesy of Joe Garland.

The Edney Family Recipe

While visiting the relatives of her father, Charlie Ledford, my mother, Janie Cook became aquainted with her cousin, Clyde Edney of Roan Mountain, Tennessee. They reminisced about stories of Uncle Steve Ledford (son of Waites Ledford) and cousin Jake Johnson making moonshine and running from the law. Their stories portrayed a past that was overshadowed by the hard times of the Great Depression. Steve operated an illegal distillery on the North Carolina side of Roan Mountain while Jake Johnson made his brew on the Tennessee side of the Roan. The stills were located near the border of North Carolina and Tennessee because the area provided an easy means of escape from the respective state and county authorities. The Johnson and Ledford moonshine recipe was known for its fine taste and potency that would cause a briar eating mule to chew up nails and spit out a barb wire fence.

Upon talking further with Clyde Edney, mom and I were privileged to get the details on how his family made moonshine. Edney stated that old timers always said that a cool spring hollow carpeted by yellow flowers called "forget-me-nots" made the prime location for a moonshine still. The presence of the yellow flowers indicated that the specific area would make a fine tasting mountain dew. Once a suitable place was found, Edney continued, the shine-maker would begin constructing his still. A homemade distillery consisted of a copper cooker being connected by a pipe to a twenty gallon thump keg and condensor. The worm was soaked in the condensor barrel which was filled with fresh, Roan Mountain spring water. In addition to the still parts, a sixty gallon oak mash barrel was situated near the cooker. With the still built, Edney discussed his family recipe.

Roan Mountain Dew was most commonly made from a mix of corn, sugar, and yeast. The Edney family recipe used about one half bushel of freshly ground corn mixed with yeast and fifty pounds of sugar. The ingredients were combined and added to a sixty gallon mash barrel filled with the spring water. According to Edney, this mixture or malt was allowed to "work off," or ferment, for about ten days. When the malt was ready or "worked off," the still parts were sealed with dough paste and a fire was built beneath the copper cooker. Upon heating the mixture in the cooker, the pressurized still forced the cooked brew through the worm and produced a powerful product. The white lightening that first came from the condenser was the most potent. Mr. Edney said that just the smell of it could get some people drunk.

Moonshine on the Charles Creek

If there was any stream in the bustling community of Glen Ayre that had 100 proof water, it would have been the Charles Creek. Flowing down from the top of Roan Mountain, the Charles Creek was an excellent place to hide an illegal distillery. Situated near several natural travel corridors, the hollow allowed for easy distribution into all of Glen Ayre, Roan Mountain, Roaring Creek and Carter County, Tennessee. At the head of the Charles Creek, the settlements of the Ledfords and Biddixs was where many a mason jar was filled with corn squeezings. In the early twenties the sound of a thump keg kept time with a crying fiddle as the rustling Charles Creek would dance wildly around massive rocks.

A picture of life on the head of the beautiful Charles Creek in 1920 would have depicted a small settlement connected to the Roan Valley Community by a forgotten path called the Mule Trail and joining Glen Ayre by a wagon trail that followed the banks of the Charles Creek to Little Rock Creek. My Great Grandfather, Anderson Waites Ledford built a house near the junction of the Mule Trail and Charles Creek which is still standing to this day. Owning more than 130 acres of land spanning the headwaters of Charles Creek and spreading into the Roan Highlands, Ledford established himself as a prominent sheep farmer. I often recall stories from my Grandpa Charlie Ledford of how he would tend to his father's sheep as they grazed on the grassy balds of the Roan. There are still a few old fence posts on the north side of Jane's Bald which serve as a reminder of the days when the locals would shepherd their flocks on the cool season grasses of the higher meadows. Although Waites was a successful rancher, his proficiency at entertaining made him a popular man within the community. Grandpa Charlie would speak of the times when brothers Waites, Steve, Taft and Wayne would pick and sing to friends that would gather on the porch of the Waites' Ledford House. The gatherings were very festive and became a common event on summer weekends. It is at these gatherings that many neighbors first became acquainted with the 100 proof water of the Charles Creek.

Mack Edwards, of whom the previous story, Roan Valley Revenge, mentions, would often pick old time banjo and play fiddle with Waites at the aforementioned gatherings. Mack was a close friend to the Ledford family. After becoming a fugitive, it was whispered that Mack would secretly visit his trusted friends. As rumors about Mack circulated, the local sheriff began to look with suspicious eyes at the Ledfords. Although authorities never caught Mack Edwards, their heightened scrutiny did result in the discovery of several moonshine distilleries in the area.

Waites began operating his still from a spring near his home in 1921. The still was expertly concealed among several large boulders in a deep cut situated near Laurel Ridge. Charlie Ledford said that Waites would grind some corn in his grist mill on Little Rock Creek and pack it in burlap feed sacks so neighbors would think he was hauling ground feed for his pasturing sheep. Grandpa Charlie, further, said that the distillery was only operated on overcast days when the clouds were covering the ridges in order to conceal the smoke from the fire that was built beneath the drum. Waites would use his boys to watch for suspicious folks while the still was cooking. The location and crafty use of the Waites' still made it a lasting fixture in a time when other stills were being smashed by the always snooping revenuers.

Though the still near Laurel Ridge was never found, Waites and his family were always walking a tight rope when transporting and distributing their Roan Mountain Dew. At the many rural concerts that were held on the stage of Waites Ledford's front porch, neighbors

Family photo of the Ledfords taken near the head of Charles Creek Road. Front Row from left to right: Taft, Rittie and Jane. Second Row: Smith, Waites and "Fiddling" Steve Ledford. Photo - Janie Ledford Cook.

and visitors from miles around would listen to the traditional tunes that would resonate through the ridges As mentioned earlier, the concerts were also the place where many a farmer got his first taste of the Ledford shine. With the fiddle crying, the banjo clanking, the guitar twanging and the high lonesome harmonies of old-time, mountain singing resonating through the hollow, the gatherings were always festive. Consequently, it was only a matter of time before someone would ask for a nip of shine and the Ledford's were happy to oblige their trusted friends. When neighbors saw people stumbling along the road to Glen Ayre, they became suspicious.

In March of 1923, the suspicion of neighbors crossed paths with the incentive of reward. The state had cracked down on bootleggers and shinemakers by offering citizens a reward for the discovery of any violations of prohibition laws. In an effort to route out illegal distilleries, a $10 reward was offered for providing the location of a still. The incentives led to heightened scrutiny of the Charles Creek by the residents of the Glen Ayre Community.

The Ledford family would hide their mason jars of shine in a metal bucket under the spring house in order to keep the whiskey cool and hidden. When folks would drink a cool jar of mountain dew on a hot summer day, it did not take much logic to figure out where the shine was being stored. As a result, the location of the jars became known to other people in the area. A warrant was written up, and the law chose to show up when Waites and his family were playing music on a Saturday evening. The sheriff went straight to the spring house and found twelve jars of moonshine. During the raid, deputies also caught Waites' sons Taft and George, along with Roscoe Edwards trying to destroy the evidence. The next day authorities brought in a search party to look for Waites's distillery. After a days search with no results, the sheriff called off the hunt. Waites, Steve, Taft and Roscoe Edwards were all taken to town for booking. Waites was sentenced to four months of hard labor while the others were warned and released. The formal charge issued against the Ledfords was a VPL (Violation of Prohibition Law) involving the possession, selling and transport of spirituous liquors. Taft, George and Roscoe Edwards were not prosecuted because they were all under the age of twenty-one. After the arrest, the Ledford's quit shinning...for a little while.

Waites and Melissa Edney Ledford lived at the head Charles Creek Road in Glen Ayre, NC. Waites is pictured holding his fiddle. Photo – Janie Ledford Cook.

After a year of slipping over to Roaring Creek to play music and drink some of the best blackberry brandy in the Appalachians; Steve, Charlie, George and Taft felt inspired to try their father's recipe once again. The discovery of the Hugh Ward Still which was downstream from the Ledford house combined with the arrest of Waites made the Charles Creek too risky a place for distillation. The Ledford boys persuaded by Will Biddix, the husband of Waites's blind sister Laura, formulated plans to construct a new distillery. According to Cleo Edwards, the new still was built near a feeder ridge adjacent to the convergence of Grassy Ridge and Yellow Mountain Pass on a spring flowing off of Cherry Orchard Ridge. The new location offered easy escape into Tennessee and the elevation of Cherry Orchard Ridge provided for a great vantage point for the watchers to look for revenuers. I cannot find any court documents stating that the Cherry Orchard Ridge Still was ever discovered. The thumping of a Ledford Still once again rang through the hollows. The Ledford's used the Cherry Orchard Still on and off throughout the hard years of the Great Depression.

With country wide prohibition ending in 1933, the availability of whiskey became more widespread. As a result, the demand for moonshine decreased as well as the number of stills. Though Mitchell County was still dry, people could legally go to neighboring "wet" counties to purchase whiskey. The Ledford's continued to make their Roan Mountain Dew for special occasions and to drink while picking and singing. The Ledford's final run-in with law occurred in 1942 when authorities once again caught Waites and his sons with illegal spirits. Waites was fined and sentenced once again to pay for his crime. The stiff fine may have caused the older Waites Ledford to sell a portion of his land, and the sentence of hard labor was said to have been a contributing factor in his death a few years later.

The First Chicken House on the Green Creek
Today one can still see the weathered siding and busted windows of the long chicken pen that is situated on the property that used to be owned by Steve Ledford. The chicken coop was one of the first in Mitchell County and was not very successful - atleast as a poultry

Photograph of chicken house that was once owned by Fiddling Steve Ledford. It is located in Glen Ayre, NC off highway 261 on Green Creek road. Photo - Allen Cook. (2019)

operation. However, providing customers with fried chicken was not what Fiddling Steve Ledford had in mind.

"Raising chickens is okay, just so ya don't put all your eggs in one basket," Steve would often laugh.

Instead of eggs, Steve would put genuine 100 proof corn mash whiskey in his basket. That was the unproven suspicion.

I have heard tales, and that may be all they were, that Steve's two stepsons hijacked a liquor truck in West Virginia and hid the goods in the hen house. The chicken operation provided a great cover because the long isles and noisy roosters made a good place to hide a truck load of whiskey. It is believed that Steve used the hen house as a bootlegging outfit for several years. The environment was very suitable for bootlegging because Steve could provide the music, whiskey and cock fighting all on the premises. In closing, the reason the chicken actually crossed the road was to visit Steve's hen house.

Through these recollections, I have only touched on the shining ventures by the Ledford's of Glen Ayre. The stories of moonshiners eluding the law in the shadow of the Roan are numerous and paint the scenery of a rich local history. A tradition of independence and fierce individuality are trademarks of the many who worked the cookers and tasted the product that became known as Roan Mountain Dew.

Chapter 9:

More About Moonshining

"What I have said about Madison County applies with equal force to Mitchell County. That county while under the reign of Whiskey, had a criminal record without parallel in the history of the state." Campaign speech of U.S. Senator, Judge Jeter Pritchard.

-Farmer and Mechanic, **North Carolina** *(1908)*

Mountain moonshiners had some legitimate reasons to ply their trade. Rural mountain towns in the early 1900s relied heavily on farming as a means of family income. When corn prices were low, many families resorted to making Mountain Dew to increase profits. In 1900, a farmer could sell 40 bushels of corn to the local mill and make a profit of around $20 or he could use the 40 bushels of corn to distill 120 gallons of corn liquor and earn a profit of $150. It was not uncommon for farmers to have a still hidden somewhere in the far reaches of their property. A farmer could transport 50 gallons of whiskey to market much easier than a wagon load of corn. While many people did not agree with the manufacture and use of illegal spirits, most tolerated the practice because it provided income to needy families.

Moonshiners were fiercely independent and resented the involvement of Government in their personal affairs. The line of thinking for most mountain people of the time was that the Government should not be able to regulate what a man does with his own corn. One IRS commissioner summed up these sentiments in a statement he made concerning the wilds of western North Carolina and east Tennessee:

"The mountains of North Carolina and Tennessee are honeycombed with stills-the owners of which annually cheat the government out of large sums of money. They contend that they have a right to sell their liquors made from their own products without government interference and are quick to resent government inspection. The whole section is in almost deadly opposition to authority in any form."
-*Marion Daily Star*, Ohio (1893)

On January 16, 1920, prohibition went into effect. Instead of illegal shine being only a matter of tax evasion, the manufacture and sale of Mountain Dew now became a violation of federal law. Local law enforcement received a mandate from the Federal Government to go after illicit whiskey. In the early 1920s, the state paid a $10 reward for the capture of any illegal distillery. Local deputies capitalized on the bounty and many stills were busted. Arrests flooded in throughout the county and officers sent conviction reports to the Mitchell County Commissioners for the approval of the $10 rewards. Old Commissioner's notes show the following still busts:

(1921) $10 reward to JB Tipton and MB Laws for arrest of Charlie Buchanan for manufacturing and retailing spirituous liquors.
(1921) $10 reward to JC Pritchard for capturing a still.
(1922) $20 reward to Frank Glenn capturing and destroying 2 stills.
(1922) $30 reward to JC Pritchard for capturing 3 stills.
(1923) $10 reward to Backus Young for capture of still.
(1923) $20 reward to IH Wright for 2 stills in Grassy Creek.
(1923) $10 IH Wright for capture of still and one Melvin Beam.
(1923) $30 BS Young for capturing 3 stills in Little Rock Creek.
(1923) $10 Wheeler Melton for capturing a still in Herrell Township.
(1924) $10 BS Young for 1 still in Little Rock Creek.
(1924) $20 MC Hoppas for 2 stills in Grassy Creek.
-*Mitchell County, NC Commissioner's Notes* (1924)

A notable still bust in the Mitchell County Moonshine Annals was the State vs. Avery Bartlett. The Avery Bartlett still was busted in the Penland area near Milk Gap in 1923 during the prohibition crackdown. Old court records gave a detailed report of the illicit distillery's location. The arresting officer located the Bartlett still at night. The deputy stated in his report that he destroyed the burner but left the still since it was late at night. He returned the next morning to find the components of the distillery had been moved during the night. Mason jars and sugar were found near the Bartlett farmhouse but no sign of the still which had been there the night before. The officers arrested Avery Bartlett and the trial was held at the Mitchell County Courthouse in Bakersville. The jury concluded that since the arresting officers had no still, there was insufficient evidence to convict Bartlett for the manufacture of spirituous liquids. The commissioners promptly passed the following ordinance:

"It is ordered by the Board of Commissioners that any officer who captures a still must produce the still to the county seat. It is further ordered that they must furnish evidence that the still has been in operation on or about the time of capture of still."
-Mitchell County, NC Commissioner's Notes (1924)

In order for a deputy to collect the $10 reward, the still had to be displayed in the town of Bakersville, probably on the steps of the courthouse.

Moonshining Mommas
The Roan holds a notorious history in its hollows and coves but perhaps the most entertaining is that of the moonshining women. A typical family set up of the early 1900s revolved around the men working in the fields and the women cooking. Old time mountain women were very well known for canning and pickling vegetables, making apple butter and preparing meals that would cause one to sell their birthright. Due to this fact, some of the best moonshine makers of Mitchell County were women.

Cal Lay and Elizabeth Cox were notorious for making the smoothest tasting moonshine around. Both women were in their elder years and well set in their ways and traditions. In the Fall of the year, when the apples were falling, the ladies made the best apple pies and apple butter in three counties. But when the corn was ripe, the women turned their attention towards another family tradition - making moonshine. The Statesville Landmark Newspaper reports the arrest of some Mitchell Moonshining Mommas:

"Cal Lay and Elizabeth Cox, 2 females of Mitchell County were convicted of retailing. They were old offenders and Judge Brawley was merciful. He suspended judgment on promise of good behavior, they are to appear at the next term of court and show that they have kept the faith. If they fail, they are to be imprisoned for 6 months."
-Statesville Record and Landmark, **North Carolina** (1897)

The common punishment for the manufacture and sell of illegal whiskey was up to one year of hard labor and/or a $100 fine. Cal Lay and Elizabeth Cox were ordered to "keep the faith." Basically the Judge let the lady's off under the promise that they would no longer make moonshine. The ladies left the courtroom and returned to Bakersville on probation. After a few years passed, Cal could no longer fight the urge to cook brew. She was caught again for moonshining and sentenced to six months in the Bakersville Jail. The Landmark follows up on the Cal Lay story:

"Governor Aycock last week pardoned Cal Lay, a woman who is serving a 12-month sentence in Mitchell County Jail. The old woman is 70 years old and was convicted of retailing liquor. She has served 4 months and her health is so broken that her release was asked for. The pardon was urged by a petition signed by many prominent citizens."
-Statesville Record and Landmark, **North Carolina** (1902)

As it is with many family traditions, once they get in your blood, it is hard for one to turn from their "wicked" ways. Moonshine making for Cal Lay came as natural as cooking a chicken on a Sunday morning. She was pardoned by the Governor upon the petition by Bakersville's "prominent citizens" and no other accounts were written concerning this moonshining Martha Stewart.

Another trio of moonshining mommas was from "the famous Rock Creek" section of Mitchell County. The Statesville Landmark recounts the story:

"OMA RIDDLE RETAILING - one month and $100, Tilda Hughes, Julia Bass and Celia Gardner - all guilty of retailing, were each given 1 year and a day in the penitentiary at hard labor and fined $100 and Johnson McKinney for illicit distilling received a similar sentence...The women mentioned are all from Mitchell County and the three sentences to the penitentiary are old offenders from the famous Rock Creek. Oma Riddle who plead guilty to retailing asked the court for mercy and her talk excited a good deal of sympathy, she said it was her first offense and promised faithfully that it would be her last, reminding District Attorney Holton when he was disposed that his mother was a woman. The woman's pleas prevailed and Judge Purnell gave her the minimum sentence for which she thanked him."
-Statesville Record and Landmark, North Carolina (1898)

The lady moonshiners of Mitchell County could sweet talk a district attorney. The women often got lighter sentences than male moonshine offenders.

Other women such as Susan Phillips out smarted the law by hiding mason jars in her knitting while the local sheriff searched her house. The story goes that while the sheriff searched Susan's house, Susan sat in her rocking chair knitting on a quilt. The quilt covered her stash of mason jars filled with Roan Mountain Dew. The Sheriff, in a gentlemanly and respectful manner apologized to Susan for the inconvenience and left. Old lady Phillips just chuckled and kept on knitting. The old time women of Mitchell were a sly fox to catch.

Perhaps an article from 1921 in the Statesville Landmark summed up the legacy of the old time moonshiner best when it stated: *"The moonshiner is a persistent cuss and industrious."* Moonshiners were a colorful part of Appalachian history and their legacy embodies the free spirit of America. The chorus to an old tune written in 1920 by Bascomb Lamar Lunceford, entitled *"Old Mountain Dew"* goes as such:

> *"Yes, they call it that old Mountain Dew.*
> *Said those who refuse it are few.*
> *While I know I've done wrong, the temptation is strong*
> *When they call for that Old Mountain Dew."*

As a child, I can remember local music makers changing the words from "old Mountain Dew" to "Roan Mountain Dew." Stories from old timers, past newspaper articles and court documents paint an interesting and recollective picture of the history and heritage of Roan Mountain Dew. Special thanks to Grandpa Charlie Ledford, Janie Ledford Cook, Clyde Edney, Joe Garland and Kenneth Ellis for contributing many of the historical facts and details about local area moonshining.

Chapter 10:

Lynching Beneath the Roan

"They then gave Bob the rope made of hemp grass, and told him he must hang English. He (Hol) begged for mercy, protesting his innocence, but the rope was tied, he and Bob still on the mule...a burly fellow in the crowd commanded, 'Bob, spur that mule.'"

-*Marion Record,* North Carolina *(1894)*

It was a bright cool evening as Ellen Carrol English walked from Roaring Creek toward her home which was a few miles north of Bakersville. The path was only about a two miles long and with several hours of daylight remaining, Ellen decided to leave Nancy English's house and walk the trail back home alone. The wagon road was well lit and went through open fields most of the way - and she felt only a little uneasy walking by herself this close to dark. As Ellen ambled past the W.O. Davis residence, her mind wondered to her husband's conversation outside Nancy's cabin.

"Why did he wait until tonight to do his business in Roaring Creek? Why is he acting so cold and short tempered?" Ellen reflected.

While cleaning for the King residence in Glen Ayre, Grovie King said that she had seen Hol in Bakersville with his former mother-in-law, Katie Wilson. Young Ellen's mind was troubled as she neared the North Toe River.

The river was running high due to recent spring rains and the roar of water made Ellen momentarily lose track of her troubled thoughts. Just ahead, Ellen Carrol English saw where the road narrowed near a steep bank. Referred to as the "Squeeze," it was the only place on the horse and wagon trail that was hidden by the forest. Ellen walked a little faster. Thinking that her two children were probably getting anxious, Mrs. English looked up to see how far the sun was from the mountain tops. As Ellen turned her head toward the Yellow Mountain Pass, she glimpsed movement in the laurel near the river bank.

Stopping to catch her breath, Ellen gave the laurel a second look and was startled momentarily when a man came out from behind a large sycamore tree. It was her husband, Hol.

Perplexed by his presence, she exclaimed, "What are you doing!"

Hol said nothing as he walked toward his recently estranged wife. Ellen turned to look over her shoulder to see if anyone else was in the woods.

As she turned away, Hol said, "You will be better off."

Perplexed, Ellen looked for discernment in Holland's face. Upon seeing the grim and uncaring expression, she realized Hol's intentions and screamed. Ellen screamed again and struggled in the damp leaves as her husband's hate and anger turned to violence. Finally, begging for mercy, Ellen watched helplessly with deep felt pain as Hol dealt a final blow.

Holland looked down at the lifeless body of Ellen. Adrenaline caused his hands and legs to shake uncontrollably. The Yellow Mountain cast a long shadow down the river bottom encompassing Hol and his wife in a shroud of darkness. Hol kept telling himself to keep a cool head, as he pulled the corpse of his wife from the road to the river's edge. The water was frigid but Hol did not feel the icy chills. He waded out near the strong currents in the middle of the North Toe River so as to let the body drift further downstream from the grizzly site of the killing. Slipping on the mossy rocks, Holland released his grip on Ellen. English watched as the force of the water carried his wife away. Ellen's body rolled over and over, bouncing and contorting against the boulders and riffles of the North Toe. Ellen's face seemed to cast a morbid glare as she disappeared beneath the turbulent spring river.

When both Ellen and Hol did not return home Sunday night, friends and family began to search the trail where Ellen was last seen. When J.G. Buchanan heard that Mr. and Mrs. English were missing, he recalled hearing faint screams by the River the previous night while walking home from W.O. Davis's cabin. Restructuring the hunt around the river where Buchanan reported to have heard the screams, a nervous search party walked along the eroded shoreline of the North Toe. Buchanan was the first to see the pale body that was washed into the roots of an old willow tree. Family members gathered around the corpse while others kept searching the rocky banks for the body of Hol. The sheriff figured that Ellen had probably slipped off the bank and drowned, but as procedure demanded, he called R.L. Prestwood- the coroner.

Upon examining the body of Ellen, Mr. Prestwood noticed that her face was bruised severely. He also noticed deep bruising around her neck. His conclusion was that Ellen had not drowned but had been murdered. The coroner's finding shocked the community.

As family gathered to mourn at Hol and Ellen's house, Hol returned home and appeared to be in a state of sorrow and anger. Swearing to avenge Ellen's death by killing the murderer, Hol went into his room to mourn. After Holland returned, everyone began to ask him questions. English said that he had been at Roaring Creek tending to business for the past two days. Upon hearing that his wife had been found dead, he rushed home. As the questions became more focused, English's alibis did not line up. With a nagging conscience, Elizabeth English, Hol's half-sister, gave Hol a hurt look as she told the crowd of family and friends that he had offered her ten dollars to kill Ellen. Upon hearing Elizabeth's statement, J.W. Ollis came forward and said that Hol English expressed that Ellen would not live long if she continued in her evil ways. Mourning turned to anger as Ellen's family accused Hol.

Holland English was promptly taken to Bakersville where he was turned over to the Mitchell County Sheriff. While Mr. English sat in jail, deputies were combing the woods around the road where Ellen disappeared. J.A. Buchanan and Jim Ollis were the first to survey the area for tracks. Buchanan got on Hol's trail in the gap near Roaring Creek. He followed the footprints which matched those of Mr. English to a sycamore tree where the defendant had stood. Buchanan then followed the tracks from the tree to within 100 yards of the place where Ellen's corpse was found. D.L. Perry also discovered the same shoe prints about a quarter mile up the river from where the body was found. He and Mitchell County Deputies measured the length and width of the tracks and found them to exactly match the shoes that Holland English had on the day of his arrest. With the evidence building, rumors began to brew in the surrounding communities.

Holland met with Colonel Bowman of whom he had retained for council. They talked for the better part of the day about the details surrounding the death of Ellen. Holland discussed the event to Bowman and the two could not make a decision on how to plea. After Col. Bowman left, Jailer Len Wilson brought Holland his supper and played cards with English and a few other inmates. It seemed to be another night as Wilson finished off some soup beans and "taders" that prisoner David Cobb was not able to stomach.

It was about nine o'clock when D.S. Elliot reported that a crowd was gathering outside of town to lynch Hol English. Len Wilson promptly summoned Beryl Stewart and Phillip Wilson to assist him in guarding the jail. Len locked Hol in the most secure cell so as to keep him out of musket range. In the cool mountain darkness the men nervously waited for the mob to arrive. Stewart watched and listened from the roof of the jail house while the two Wilson brothers secured the door. Four hours passed and the jailers began to wonder if the mob had disbanded.

About two o'clock, Beryl Stewart came down from the roof looking like he had seen a ghost. He said that he saw torches and heard a lot of voices coming up the street towards the jail. Len Wilson looked out the window and estimated the crowd to be over two hundred in number. The three men nervously readied their firearms for the upcoming show down.

As the crowd gathered around the Bakersville Jail, a man unknown to Len yelled, "We've come to get Holland and don't want to see anyone else 'git' hurt."

Wilson replied, "Let the courts do their job and go on home."

The man then said that the crowd was going to take Holland and hang him at the place where he killed his wife. Holland seemed to know the fate that awaited him and told Wilson to release him to the mob so nobody would get hurt. The jailer refused. The light of flames danced on the faces of the men and the white paint of the jail when there came a shout from a burley looking man in the middle of the mob saying, "burn'em out!"

The three jailers pleaded with the mob to no avail. The conglomeration's emotions boiled high and patience grew thin. At 2:30 a.m., the angry crowd began to beat on the door of the jail and threatened to use dynamite if the jailers did not relinquish Mr. English. The jailers stood firm.

Suddenly, with a loud crack, the door gave way to the force of the mob. The crowd rushed in and restrained the three men guarding the prisoners. Grabbing the key from Mr. Wilson, a man made his way towards Holland's cell. Screams were heard when the men grabbed English and roughly pushed his face into the plank floor. English's hands were tied as he pleaded his innocence to the men. Ten men escorted Holland out of the jail. When he appeared, a large shout went out from the crowd. Holland English was then led over to a mule where his 12-year-old brother-in-law, Bob Carrol, brother to Ellen Carrol, helped his "Uncle Hol" saddle up for a final ride.

The moans and cries of a man staring death in the eyes pierced the night. The sight of the doomed rider had an eerie effect on the once loud crowd. Everyone was silent and sadistically intrigued as a procession of over 200 people followed a condemned man on a mule led by a boy. The mob grew in size as Hol went down the road towards Roan Mountain Church.

A suitable tree was found on Milt Buchanan's land to accomplish the deed. The crowd gathered around the mule as Hol watched with terror. Milt begged the men not to hang Holland on his land. The mule kept walking. The mob proceeded up the road towards Moses Young's stable and prepared to hang English on a buckeye tree but decided against it because there was not a high enough limb. With dawn approaching, the lynch mob drifted over to one of Moses's pastures and opened a gate that led into an apple orchard.

A bearded man led the mule beneath a stout branch. There was no rope, only a six foot stretch of hemp cord which was tied to a branch that was accustomed to bearing the weight of apples - not a grown man. English was granted fifteen minutes to pray. There were three preachers in the crowd and they all prayed for the sentenced man.

Bob Carrol sat on the same mule as his brother-in-law and said, "Now Uncle Hol, I am going to tie the other end of this rope around your neck."

English was silent as little Bob slipped the noose around the neck of the man he referred to as Uncle Hol. Anticipation and tension rose in the mob.

A burley man then said, "Bob, spur that mule."

Bob Carrol spurred the mule and left his brother-in-law suspended in the air. Because the fall did not break his neck, Hol's death resulted from strangulation. Upon seeing the lifeless man sway in the early morning light, everyone walked briskly towards their homes.

When dawn spread a dim light over the field of Moses Young, Hat Byrd and some of his relatives found Hol in the apple tree and reported the location to the authorities. The coroner made an inquest into the lynching but found no witnesses with a definite identification of the participants involved in the killing.

After many private citizens and the town of Bakersville refused to donate land for English's grave site, a citizen named Mr. Love stepped forward. Hol was buried on the property of Mr. Love in the middle of his blackberry patch. Mr. Love said that because Hol's legal rights failed, he felt that the spirit of English had a moral right to protect his blackberry patch from intruders. To this day Hol's spirit still haunts the blackberry patch. A large rock on a dirt mound marks the grave of the last lynching beneath the Roan.

Chapter 11:

More About the Lynching

"On the 25th of March 1894, Hol English, a well-known tough character of Mitchell County, committed a most dastardly crime - that of murdering his wife."

-*Marion Record*, North Carolina *(1894)*

I n 1894 Holland English was lynched outside of Bakersville, North Carolina. Researching the coroner's inquest and old newspaper clippings revealed the details leading to his death.

The Victim
The victim Ellen Carrol English was found dead on the banks of the North Toe River three days after being reported as missing near a community in Avery County, North Carolina called Frank. The coroner's report revealed that Mrs. English had been beaten to death and then thrown in the river to disguise the brutal killing. Upon the coroner's findings a thorough investigation of the crime scene revealed footprints matching the size and shoe type of Holland English. With a suspect in mind authorities began to build a case against Mr. English.

Ellen was listed on the 1890 census as a stepdaughter to W.H. Ollis. She had two brothers named James and Bob Carrol. Little Bob Carrol was said to have spurred the mule of "Uncle Hol." Though Holland and Ellen were not closely related, a linkage can be made on the basis of in-laws. When Holland was implicated in the death of Ellen,

117

tempers flared in the families and settlements surrounding Roaring Creek.

The Accused

Holland English was first accused for the murder of his wife Ellen English by his half-sister, Elizabeth English. Her accusation set into motion the State's gathering of testimonies and evidence that became the basis of a strong case against Mr. English. Unfortunately, the justice system never got the chance to litigate the case due to Holland's date with a string of hemp.

Holland English was assumed to be the son of Matilda English Ledford. I found no records of Holland's father. It was believed by some that Hol's father worked at the Cloudland Hotel and may have been an ex-slave from Marion, NC. Other locals said that Hol's father may have been of French Creole descent due to his blue eyes. Before he married Ellen Carrol, Hol was married to Sealie Wilson of whom bore him four children. Roscoe Edwards said that Holland built a home on the Charles Creek in Glen Ayre that was later bought by Doanie Speaks. After divorcing Sealie, it was rumored that Sealie's mother, Katie Wilson, wanted English to marry Hattie Wilson, Sealie's younger sister. When Ellen and Hol began to have problems, it is believed that Hol started to entertain thoughts of marrying Hattie. With a motive in place, the demise of Ellen began to formulate in the mind of Holland - or did it?

Damning Testimonies

The written statement of Elizabeth English went as follows:

"Elizabeth English being sworn says Defendant Holland English said to me at Nance English's, I will give you $10.00 if you will kill Ellen. I told him I would do no such a thing. Then he said if I would not do it, he would do it himself. He also said that I could be passing along by a hole of water and push her in and nobody would mistrust me. He said this on or about Sunday, March 1894." -Elizabeth English attest W.H. Ollis
-Mitchell County, NC Coroner's Inquest (1894)

118

The chilling testimony of Elizabeth English stated that Holland offered her $10 to kill his wife Ellen English. The above photo is the actual recorded account from the 1894 coroner's inquest. Photo – Allen Cook. (1997)

Samuel Keller sets the scene of Ellen English's final hours with Hol:

"Samuel Keller being sworn says-- I was with defendant Hol English on Sunday March 25, 1894. The deceased was with Defendant talking near the chimney corner. They talked for a while and came in the house. Deceased started to go and defendant said you had better go across the Grassy Ridge. Deceased said she could not at that time of the day. Defendant said when are you to leave. I am satisfied the boots that Hol English now has on made the tracks leading to and from where the deceased was found in the Toe River. Defendant said (when leaving) he had to stop on Roaring Creek and had business to tend. -Samuel Keller

-Mitchell County, NC Coroner's Inquest (1894)

119

After Ellen English left the above mentioned house, she was murdered and thrown into the North Toe River. In the locality near the killing, J.G. Buchanan reported hearing a lady screaming by the river. It was downstream of the reported area in Buchanan's testimony where authorities recovered the body of Mrs. English.

On March 28, three days after the murder, Hol was taken into custody by the Bakersville Sheriff's Department. J.W. Ollis, a brother-in-law to Nancy English, recalls some of the events that transpired upon the arrest of Mr. English.

"J.W. Ollis being sworn says,
I next saw Holland English on March 28 under arrest. I heard English March 24 curse the deceased and say that he would not live with the deceased to save her from hell and the way she was doing, she would not live long." - J.W. Ollis

Perhaps the most damning evidence to surface was the tracks that were found in the area where Ellen was murdered. Shoe prints in the woods revealed that Ellen had been stalked prior to her death. The footprints in the muddy banks of the North Toe matched those of Mr. English in both tread and size.

"J.A. Buchanan being sworn says,
I went to gap near Roaring Creek (to look for Holland's tracks) and found a track which I am certain was made by the boot English now has on. I came about 30 yards from the gap and found where defendant had stood for some time under a tree. I tracked it from there to within 100 yards of where deceased was found. I saw and measured the track where it had left the river and found it corresponded with the tracks in the gap." -J.A. Buchanan

"D.L. Perry after being sworn says,
I measured tracks near where deceased was found. They measured 11.25 inches and looked as if they were the tracks of a man. The track looked as if it had been made by a run-down boot. Then I went and measured the foot of the defendant and it measured 11.25 inches; the

same as the track. His boots looked as if they had made the track...Heel corresponded with defendant." -D.L. Perry
-Mitchell County, NC Coroner's Inquest (1894)

The Bakersville Mob

On the night of April 2, 1894 at two o'clock in the morning, an angry mob gathered outside the town of Bakersville. Around 10:00 p.m., Mitchell County Deputy Phillip Wilson heard reports of a gathering outside of town. Len Wilson and Beryl Stuart came to the jail around 10:30 that night to assist Phillip in the event that the gathering turned hostile. With the stage set, the statements of the three jailers' best depict the happenings on that early spring night:

"Phillip Wilson after being sworn says,
Yesterday evening I was notified by D.S. Elliot that there may be a crowd in that night to lynch Holland English. I summonsed Beryl Stewart and Len Wilson to assist me in guarding the jail. I set up till midnight and then laid down and went to sleep. At 2:00 I was awakened by a noise at the door. I got up and put on my clothes and went to the door and asked who was there. I was answered, 'Brown Burleson with a prisoner, and I want to put him up.' I said I don't think that is him. He said that it was him and to let him in cause he's getting cold. I opened the door and found the land full of men. I shut the door at once and told them I wanted to have a talk with them before they got in the jail. They said then that there was no use for any talk and that they had come for Holland English and was going to have him. I said let's consider the matter and let the law take its course as I did not believe in lynching a man. They said open the door or we will throw dynamite under the house and blow it up. I told them to throw it as I would not open the door. Someone in the crowd said light it and throw it under if he don't open the door. I refused to open the door and then someone struck the door with a stick of wood and broke it open. They came in and demanded the keys of which I refused to give them. Someone came up to me and put his hand in my pocket and took the keys, who he was I do not know. They opened the door and went in and tied [Holland English] and brought him out. The

121

deceased called for his hat. I got it and gave it to him. He called on me and someone else to go with him. One of the crowd said they would take him to where he murdered his wife and lynch him there. They tied a rope around his neck and put him on a horse. I suppose there were about 100 persons in the crowd and about 1 dozen of them in the jail." - Phillip Wilson

"Len Wilson says,
I was at the jail when the mob came March 31 at two o'clock. I heard someone call at the jail. I got up and asked what they wanted. They said they were Brown Burleson's crew. They said they wanted Holland English. I told them they could do better things. They said if the door was not opened they would burn it down. I went to the other side of the house and found a crowd there trying to get in the window. Then they said light that dynamite and put it under the house. I told Wilson the jailer not to open the door and if they wanted to break in let them do so. Then they hit the door and broke it down. They then came in and deceased hollered a few times. Then I left and they came after me and stopped me until they got him out. I don't know any of the crowd. None of them wore masks. Deceased was tied when they brought him out. They asked me to get a rope and I refused. One of the crowd got a halter rope off a bridle and put him on a horse and left with him. I think one of John Davis' boys was in the crowd. It was not Tom Davis but a younger one." -Len Wilson

"Beryl Stewart says,
I was requested by the jailer to sit up with him which I did. Len Wilson came to me and said they have come - I heard someone knock on the door. They asked Wilson to open the door. He refused. They was on both sides of the door. They said if he did not open the door, they would break in in a few moments. They broke the door in and came in. Said we came for Hol English and will have him in spite of Hell.

Copy of Coroner's Inquest stating that "Ellen English came to her death at the hands of one Holland English by violence." Note that the inquest assumed Holland English killed Ellen English before he got a chance to stand trial. Photo – Allen Cook. (2019)

They called for the keys. Don't know how they got the keys. They opened the door. Someone said to Hol to confess. Don't know if he did or not. Could not hear for the fuss. One man said bring him out we'll make him confess. They had him tied around the arms--he said it was too tight; they slackened it. Took him out, I did not go out. 12 or 10 in the house. The door they broke was to the kitchen. The hall door was not closed. I did not know any of the crowd." -Beryl Stewart **-Mitchell County, NC Coroner's Inquest** (1894)

It is difficult to believe that the three jailers did not know any of the crowd. There were at least 100 people gathered around the jail. I believe that the jailers may have been a little blind to their friends and neighbors who showed up in the pre-dawn darkness. On the other hand, I'm sure there is and was a legitimate case that the darkness inhibited the positive identification of any participant in the lynching.

The Lynching of Holland English

The testimonies in the coroner's inquest provide interesting information on the final minutes of English. An eye witness to the procession recalls the account of the lynching:

"John Davis Jr. after being sworn says,
I saw a crowd coming down the road by Roan Mountain Church. I came on after the crowd to the jail. I heard something strike the jail door and saw it fly open. I stepped up into the jail door and heard someone say hang him and be done with it. I saw them bring a man out of the jail. They carried him up Cane Creek to Milt Buchanan's. There they tried to hang him and Buchanan begged them not to hang him there so they went on up to Moses Young's stable and prepared to hang him there but did not. Then they went on up above the stable to a gate and passed through the gate into the field. There they hanged him to an apple tree. I don't know any man who was in the crowd that did the hanging." -John Davis Jr.
-Mitchell County, NC Coroner's Inquest (1894)

When the gray light of dawn spread its dim glow on the scene of the lynching, the night's activities were revealed to the awakening eyes of the community. L.C. Byrd was first to discover the suspended body. His statement is as follows:

L.C. Byrd says,
I know deceased to be Hol English. Hat Byrd, Sam McKinney, three boys and myself found him just before sun up hanging in an apple tree in Moses Young's field. Many tracks there as if there had been a large crowd there. Saw larger crowd near town and supposed they had deceased and had hung him. I suppose there was 100 men in the crowd. -L.C. Byrd
-Mitchell County, NC Coroner's Inquest (1894)

The records that were found in the coroner's inquest reflect the most reliable information about the death of Ellen and lynching of Holland because it is from sworn statements and eye witness accounts. I feel that the above coroner's inquest accounts are the most accurate record

124

of the Holland English incident, but newspaper clippings from the time of the lynching tell the story as it was heard in the community. The next two accounts are from the *Marion Record*.

Judge Lynch in Mitchell County

"A Hank of Hemp - Hol English Mobbed for Murdering his Wife - Taken from Jail Sunday Morning by a Mob of Two Hundred. On Sunday evening, the 25 of March, Hol English, a well-known tough character of Mitchell County, committed a most dastardly crime - that of murdering his wife. Mrs. English, nee Ellen Carrol, was married to Hol English about a year ago, but they separated a short time after their marriage. Recently, English has been visiting his former wife occasionally for the purpose, it now appears, of taking her life, in order that he could marry another woman.

On the evening he accomplished this terrible deed he called at the house where she lived, near North Toe River, a few miles to the north of Bakersville, and induced her to walk with him. The couple did not return that evening and neighbors instituted a search for them on Tuesday morning.

Upon inquiry being made, some people who lived near the bank of the river said they had heard what seemed to be the screams of a woman after dark the evening before, but it was late and they had paid little attention to it. Acting on this information, a search was made along the river, which resulted in the finding of the body of Mrs. English, in the river. It is believed from the bruises on the body that English had beaten her to death and then thrown the body into the water in order to cover up the hideous crime.

After the news of the murder spread throughout the neighborhood, English came upon the scene and appeared very indignant. He swore he would avenge the murder by killing the person who committed it, if he could be found. In the meantime, a neighboring woman made a statement to the crowd who were assembled at the home of the dead woman to the effect that English had offered her $10.00 to poison Mrs. English. English was promptly arrested by the crowd and

125

carried to Bakersville Jail. Other evidence was found also which satisfied the people of that community that he was guilty of and on last Sunday morning a mob of 200 men went to the jail in the quiet little village of Bakersville, took English out about a mile from town on the Cranberry Road, and with a skein of hemp as a substitute for a rope, hanged him to a 'sour apple tree.'

English was said to be slightly tainted with Negro blood, but his wife was white. He bore a bad reputation. Mrs. English leaves one child."
-Marion Record, North Carolina (1894)

A North Carolina Lynching
"They had no rope, but hanged him all the same. A special from Marion, NC says Holland English was taken from jail at Bakersville and hanged by a mob of two hundred men on Sunday morning at 3 o'clock for the murder of his wife whom he killed to marry another woman. He first offered his half-sister $10.00 to poison his wife. A flax hank was used to hang English, no rope being at hand.

'More about the Hanging' From an eye-witness we have it that Hol English was hanged in Mitchell County two weeks ago by a boy named Bob Carroll, who was under thirteen years of age. Bob is a brother to English's late wife, whom he murdered. When the mob reached Bakersville Jail, the jailer and his guards refused, but the mob was about two hundred strong and they threatened to use dynamite, and the jailer agreed to surrender the prisoner. They procured the victim and tied his hands behind him and placed him on a mule behind little Bob Carroll, to take his last ride on earth.

When the mob reached the orchard near the church on the Cranberry Road 1-3/4 mile from Bakersville, about 3:30 Sunday morning, they halted, ordered little Bob Carroll to ride up under an apple tree, and English's feet were tied together, he was still sitting on the mule behind Bob Carroll.

They then gave Bob the rope made of hemp grass, and told him he must hang English. The boy tied the rope to a limp hanging above his head, and holding the other end in his hand, said 'Now, Uncle Hol, I am going to tie the other end around your neck,' and proceeded to do so.

English was given fifteen to minutes to pray. There were three preachers present, and all prayed for the doomed man. He begged for mercy, protesting his innocence, but the rope was tied, he and Bob still on the mule, and when fifteen minutes expired, a burly fellow in the crowd commanded, 'Bob, spur that mule.' Bob spurred the mule and left his brother-in-law suspended in the air between the limb of the tree and the ground. His feet lacked only four inches touching the ground. The fall did not break his neck, but his death resulted from strangulation.

We also learn that English's wife had two little children, whom she left at home the evening he murdered her...reported that he confessed the crime to Col. Bowman, whom he had retained as counsel".
-*Marion Record,* **North Carolina** (1894)

In order to draw the Holland English story to a close, I will recount the story of his burial.

The Linville River Railroad.
Between Montezuma and Pineola the railroad passes the handsome new home of T.A. Love, Esq., late of Bakersville. One of the most worthy things we ever knew Mr. Love to do, occurred the day after Hol English was lynched for the murder of his wife.

After many private citizens, as well as the town, had refused to give ground for English's grave, Mr. Love came to the rescue. He had a Blackberry Patch two miles from town, where intruders gathered all his pie stuffing in spite of all the notices he had posted on trees and fence stakes for their protection.

He said that he would give the land provided English were buried in the center of that briar patch. The offer was accepted, and the next morning after the burial, a report was circulated that something like a spread newspaper had been seen to rise from the grave to a great height then stopping, it slowly descended to the place from which it came.

This was construed as a token that English's spirit could not depart that place, but would ever remain to haunt those who assayed to intrude upon Mr. Love's brambles. Mr. Love says that after his legal rights failed, he had a moral right to protect his wild fruit, because had it not been due to laziness, every freeholder in and around Bakersville could have had a briar thicket of his own.
-The Messenger, **North Carolina** (1897)

And so, we cinch the noose on the Holland English Story.

Chapter 12:

Final Trip to the Land of Clouds

"The rescuers found him unconscious, standing erect in a snow-drift, his mouth and eves open."
-*Evening Star*, Washington D.C. *(1889)*

A chilly damp breeze pushed moisture burdened clouds against the evergreen ridges of the Roan. Veiled in a soft white mist, the rambling breeze shook the lonesome pines causing them to whisper a somber tune. The age-old mountain harmony stirred a primal sense of urgency in a wandering soul.

A little winded, tired and slightly sweating, an aging ex-sheriff, C.C. McKinney leaned on his walking stick and studied the woods surrounding an old familiar trail. It was the last day of autumn and a few days before Christmas – December 20, 1888. Completing his trip up the mountain to a high elevation water source called the Iron Springs, the old mountaineer rested and reflected on his first trip to the springs. Lost in the fog and lulled by the whispers of the pines, the sheriff reminisced of a day from his youth when his father led the way up the old path to the springs. His dad called them the "orange" springs partly because the clay and silt in the springhead had an orange color from the native iron deposits and partly because "iron" and "orange" was pronounced about the same way in the local dialect.

Feeling a pronounced chill and seeing the signs of an impending weather change, C.C. pulled together a mix of dead fir needles, birch shavings and dry twigs to build a fire by a large shelter rock. As the warmth of the campfire penetrated his hard leather hands, old Sheriff McKinney shifted to the chore of gathering more firewood and yelling for critters. He was looking for his hogs. It was customary to let hogs and livestock run loose in the fall so they could fatten up on the abundant chestnuts and hawthorn berries that littered the high elevation backwoods. After a gluttonous day of rooting out leaf covered chestnuts, C.C.'s hogs usually ended up near the Iron Springs for water and a mud bath. Calling and searching to no avail, McKinney gave up his hunt for the lost swine and shifted his priorities toward eating and staying warm.

A tin cup for drinking spring water, a half full Mason jar of applejack whiskey, a hard cake of corn bread and a single potato all wrapped up in a canvas tarp was all that he packed for the day trip. As the "tader" cooked in the coals of the fire, C.C. took a sip of the whiskey and remembered days from his youth when he and his dad would dig ramps and pick branch lettuce near the springs. After a day of digging, they would sit under the large shelter rock and fry fatback and ramps in a skillet over an open fire. His dad would always drizzle the hot grease from the frying pan over the branch lettuce to complete the backwoods treat. C.C. wished he had some ramps and branch lettuce. He wished his dad was still alive. A random gust of cold wind shivered C.C.'s body and snapped his mind back to the present. The old lawman stuck his knife into the cooked "tader" and took another sip of applejack.

As night closed in, the rambling breeze that once serenaded so beautifully through the pines turned into a hissing gale. The soft white fog that enveloped the high mountain spring head froze to the trees - intricately outlining the woods in a crystalline layer of ice. Sheriff McKinney knew he was in for a long, cold night. With rocks and leaves stacked against the windward side of his shelter rock and a hot burning fire, McKinney figured to hike out at first light.

Resolved to keep the fire going all night, McKinney made no plans to sleep. Huddled into a wool coat and covered by a canvas tarp, the

130

mountaineer got comfortable as he waited out the sudden storm. A few hours after dark, heavy snow driven by the unrelenting winds piled up outside his shelter. The old sheriff had rationed just enough firewood to make it to daybreak.

Morning light spread fast through the snow-covered Roan Mountain woods. The wind had finally died back to a shifty cold breeze as billions of tiny flecks of blew snow shimmered in the sky around the first rays of sun. Off to the west, distant pink clouds looked to bring another round of snow. The sheriff was shivering and needed to get to shelter. He gauged his options. Everything was slick. The leeward side of all the ridges and bluffs held deep snow drifts. A layer of ice covered by snow was a dangerous combination for a long downhill hike. The ridges were frozen but the snow was not deep since most of it had blown into the valleys. McKinney reasoned that his best and closest way out was to continue up the trail along the wind-swept ridge to the Cloudland Hotel.

After a breakfast cup of heated spring water spiked with a shot of homemade applejack, McKinney threw the last log on the dying fire and warmed himself before starting the one-hour uphill hike to the Cloudland. His aching body was stiffened by the cold and from being hunched over the fire all night. As the final log burned out, McKinney hit the trail. Finding hogs was the last thing on the ex-sheriff's mind as he found his pace. McKinney knew that he had to start moving to generate heat in order to get warm. He began a brisk walk up the trail towards the Cloudland. As he neared the top, the sheriff cut a set of tracks in the snow and wondered who else was unfortunate enough to be caught in the snowstorm. Scanning the frozen landscape, McKinney caught movement up the trail of a solitary boy carrying a shotgun struggling through a snow drift. The old sheriff caught up to the boy.

"Son, what are you doing out here in all this cold?" McKinney's gruff voiced barked.

131

"My momma works at the Cloudland and I was out tracking rabbits in the new snow. Reckon I got turned around," the young'un shivered as he explained.

"Well I'm headed up to the Cloudland, you may as well follow me out," the ex-sheriff grunted. "What's your name boy?"

The boy was about 15-years-old and replied, "Lum Ramsey."

"Well Lum, let's get out of this shit'n cold place," McKinney mumbled as he pulled the boy out of the drift.

The two began to navigate through the snow up the ridge. Fir limbs bowing to the weight of ice and snow made the trail almost indiscernible. Tired and sweating, a cold wind began to blast Lum and McKinney. The distant pink clouds that C.C. noted earlier that morning had arrived sooner than expected. The clouds enveloped the ridge in a frozen white mist. Visibility was down to feet. With the trail obscured by frozen clouds, McKinney and Ramsey knew they were in a tough spot. Wind chills were becoming dangerous as a reinforcement of cold Canadian air collided with the already frozen mountain. McKinney led the young'un in the direction of the Cloudland. They were off the trail but in the general area near the Cloudland wagon road. Lum was not dressed for the cold and was beginning to shake uncontrollably. The wind was cutting through him like knives and hypothermia was becoming a concern. McKinney was cold but better suited for the weather with his heavy wool jacket and canvas tarp used as a windbreaker.

"Keep walking! If you stop, you'll freeze! Now you keep moving boy," C.C. sounded like a strict mountain father talking to a stubborn son.

The old sheriff took the lead as the two made a straight route for the crest of Roan Mountain. Watching out for Lum, trudging through frozen clouds, and navigating slick terrain caused the old sheriff to remember the time when he and his father had to push through the thick clouds to the bald on Roan Ridge. He was glad to have his father back then to guide him up the mountain.

The last part of the trek seemed to take forever. C.C. and Lum were almost to the road but the final stretch was through a snow covered mix of sapling firs and rhododendron thicket. The snow and saplings hid ice-covered rocks and fallen trees. Focused on getting Lum to safety, McKinney lost footing when he mis-stepped into an ice-covered crevice hidden by the snow. The hammering jolt of the fall snapped the old sheriff's brittle bone when his ankle twisted into the rocks.

Temporarily numbed by the extreme cold, a dull pain moved up his leg. His ankle could not support his weight. McKinney gathered back his senses and tried to keep moving. He tripped and stumbled in the snow on his injured ankle. Lum tried to help the old sheriff walk, but the 15-year-old was showing signs of exposure and barely able to walk himself. McKinney brushed the snow off the ground and sat down to rest. Settling down, McKinney tried to start a fire but frozen fumbling hands, gusting winds, and ice-covered kindling made the effort a futile cause.

"Son, fire a shot with that gun in case somebody's nearby," McKinney commanded.

Lum fired two shots into the icy, wind driven fog. Lum had only one cartridge left. Both man and boy were not moving and the cold was bearing down. The sheriff made the final call.

"Son, these woods should break into a bald just up yonder," C.C. pointed. "Once you get up there, walk that bald until you find the hotel. Take this here or you're gonna freeze to death," McKinney demanded as he handed him his wool jacket.

"No sir," Lum protested. "You'll surely freeze to death."

"Don't you back talk me! Get your ass up that hill or we both gonna freeze to death!" C.C. snapped.

McKinney rolled out his canvas tarp and wrapped himself tight. Lum helped the old mountaineer get situated and out of the wind as best he could. McKinney convinced the boy that he would be okay. Lum carefully climbed out of the boulder choked death trap. Lum left the shotgun with the sheriff. The old sheriff watched as the boy climbed towards the ridge and then faded into the frozen clouds.

A young boy covered in snow and ice broke out of the thicket and onto a snowy expanse. A gust of wind slammed into Lum as he fought through a snow drift and crested the windswept, frozen bald. Through the icy fog, Lum could see the outline of the horse and buggy trail that the summer guests of the Cloudland Hotel used to leisurely traverse their way to and from the ridgetop resort. Lum struggled towards the Cloudland. Completely snow covered with his clothes stiffened by frozen sweat, the boy could barely climb the steps. With his last gathering of strength, Lum stumbled against the door making a loud thump as he fell forward.

The caretakers of the Cloudland heard the young lad's commotion on the porch and quickly carried him inside. As he came to his senses, he told of how McKinney led him to safety and pleaded for permission to lead a search crew. His mother forbade the hypothermic 15-year-old to leave.

A few hundred feet below the Roan Ridge, an old man shivered. To ease the pain and numbness in his leg, C.C. finished off the mason jar of whiskey. The false warmth lulled him into drowsiness. The delicate sound of the wind through a thousand, frozen pine needles reminded McKinney of his mother's lullabies when he was a young child. He pictured a familiar rock fireplace and his mother's soothing voice, singing familiar hymns while his father stoked the fire. His mom and dad had went on to Heaven - both falling ill many years back. Eyes growing heavy, the winter wind softly sang the sheriff to sleep. As his father had led him up the mountain on many occasions,

McKinney had led Lum to safety. To the serenade of ice-covered pines, the old sheriff stepped into a frozen cloud which dipped low to the mountain. McKinney's mother was waiting for him. His Father led the way.

A woman and her son staying at the Cloudland knew C.C. In a buggy loaded with blankets, they made a dash to get the old sheriff out. Able to follow Lum's tracks in the snow, they quickly made it back to C.C.'s location. It was too late. McKinney had drifted off into a permanent sleep.

The death of C.C. McKinney shocked the community. One old timer told the story he had heard from his father. He recounted the day they brought C.C.'s body off the mountain in a wagon. The deceased sheriff's body was covered with a tarp, but since C.C. was a tall man, his feet protruded out of the back of the wagon. It was an eerie sight as the wagon passed by. The account of McKinney's tragic death also circulated throughout local newspapers and around the country:

North Carolina is Having Winter.
A Raleigh. N.C. special to the New York World says: Although the winter here has been remarkably mild, there has been rough weather west of the Blue Ridge. Ex-Sheriff C.C. McKinney, of Mitchell County, was frozen to death at night on Roan Mountain while at a height of over 6,000 feet and near Cloudland Hotel. He was with a young man named Columbus Ramsey. The latter made a desperate attempt to save McKinney and himself had a narrow escape from death. Ice formed in his eyes and mouth and his arms and legs were badly frozen as he crawled upon his hands and knees in the snow. The rescuers found him unconscious, standing erect in a snow-drift his mouth and eves open. The same night Charlie Swan, eighteen years old, was found frozen near Bakersville, Mitchell County. He had gone after whiskey and was returning, when he fell from a precipice into an immense drift of snow.
-Evening Star, **Washington D.C.** (1889)

135

In the *Shadow* of the
ROAN

Froze to Death.
A few days before Christmas Mr. C.C. McKinney, the defeated candidate for the Legislature in Mitchell County, in company with his friend, Columbus Ramsey, left his home on Little Rock Creek to go to the Roan and before reaching the hotel on top of the mountain, McKinney observed to his friend, that he was getting cold and numb and could not go any farther. His friend worked with him for some time, but to no effect. The ground was covered with snow and it was impossible to get him farther without help. He left him alone and went to the hotel, which was some distance off and a kind lady, with a little boy, armed with a supply of blankets, started to where McKinney was left by his friend; but on arriving at the place the poor fellow was stiff and cold in death. By this time McKinney's friend having been exposed so long in the snow and cold began to feel the same sensation, when the lady wrapped him in blankets and with great effort succeeded in getting him to the hotel, and with the aid of blankets and fresh spring water, they brought him to his natural feeling and today he owes his existence to the timely aid rendered by this heroic lady, and boy.
-The Standard, **North Carolina** (1889)

Latest News Items.
The Bakersville Democrat says that Mr. McKinney, late Democratic candidate for the Legislature in Mitchell county, who was found frozen to death on the Roan Mountain a few weeks ago, had been living a very intemperate life, which accounts for his untimely death...

The Bakersville Democrat says: A few nights ago Charley Swan, a lad of 18 years, was found dead on Cane creek, three miles from Bakersville. It appears that he had gone out after whiskey and was returning, when he fell from a dangerous precipice, breaking his neck and mutilating his body.
-Weekly State Chronicle, **North Carolina** (1889)

Sheriff C.C. McKinney lived and died in the shadow of the Roan. As a lawman of Mitchell County, McKinney faced death numerous times and managed to beat the odds. For some reason, I can't help but think that the old sheriff was ready to take his final trip to the land of clouds.

We locals refer to Roan Mountain as "The Roan." Stories from its grassy ridges and fir forests are firmly rooted into the life and heritage of the mountaineers who live in its shadow. Through the generations, many have tried to develop and tame the mountain and its people, but none have succeeded. Like the Roan, those who are truly connected to the mountain continue to hold steadfastly their independence, traditions and values.

May your Roan roots run deep.

-Allen

References

A North Carolina Lynching. (1894, April 13). *Marion Record*, p. 1.

Above the Clouds. (1879, June 14). *Knoxville Daily Chronicle, 10*, p. 1. Retrieved from https://chroniclingamerica.loc.gov/lccn/sn85033437/1879-06-14/ed-1/seq-1/

Baker, L. (Ed.). (1863, October 7). Rebel Accounts of the Battle of Chickamauga. *The Daily Register, 1*(76), p. 1. Retrieved from https://chroniclingamerica.loc.gov/lccn/sn86092517/1863-10-07/ed-1/seq-1/

Bakersville Enterprise. (1894, April 11). *The Wilmington Messenger*, p. 3.

Clark, C. &. (Ed.). (1897, October 26). End of Federal Court. *Statesville Record And Landmark, 24*(27), p. 3.

Clark, C. &. (Ed.). (1898, April 22). The Federal Court. *Statesville Record And Landmark, 24*(77), p. 4.

Cloudland Hotel On top of Roan Mountain. (1900). *University of North Carolina at Chapel Hill Archive*. Memphis, Tennessee: Press of SC Toof and Co.: Cloudland Hotel. Retrieved from https://archive.org/details/cloudlandhotel6300clou/page/n3

Condensed News. (1895, February 14). *The Comet*(555), p. 2.

Coroner's Inquest of Holland English (Mitchell County April 1, 1894).

Craig, L. (1908, December 3). Mr. Linney Collapsed. *The News-Herald, XXIV*(35), p. 1.

Daniels, J. (Ed.). (1889, February 8). Latest News Items. *Weekly State Chronicle, 19*(1), p. 3.

Froze to Death. (1889, January 18). *The Standard, 2*, p. 2.

Haldeman, W. (1866, January 23). The Campaign in Kentucky. General Bragg's Official Report. *Louisville Daily Courier*, p. 1.

Harris, W. H. (Ed.). (1921, August 9). Alleged Desperado Still at Liberty. *The Charlotte Observer*, p. 3.

J.T. Wilder, Bv't - Brig General. (Photographed between 1861 and 1865, printed later). *None*. Retrieved from https://www.loc.gov/item/95503098/

Judge Lynch in Mitchell County. (1894, April 6). *Marion Record, 3*(3), p. 1.

Judge Pritchard on Prohibition. (1908, March 17). *Farmer and Mechanic, 30*(37), p. 1.

Mitchell County NC Commissioner's Notes. (1924). Bakersville, North Carolina, Mitchell County.

North Carolina Is Having Winter. (1889, January 14). *Evening Star, 74*, p. 3. Retrieved from https://chroniclingamerica.loc.gov/lccn/sn83045462/1889-01-14/ed-1/seq-3/

North Carolina Section. (1894, April 11). *The Wilmington Messenger*, p. 3.

North Carolina Tragedy. (1907, July 1). *The Salt Lake Herald, 2*. Salt Lake City, UT.

Photo taken by Allen Cook. (2019). Bakersville, North Carolina.

Plyler. (1909, September 21). Mountain Climb into Cloudland. *The Farmer and Mechanic, 33*, p. 9. Retrieved from https://chroniclingamerica.loc.gov/lccn/sn99061556/1909-09-21/ed-1/seq-1/

Reams, R. (Ed.). (1887, July 23). Among the Clouds. *Southern Standard, 8*(35), p. 4. Retrieved from https://chroniclingamerica.loc.gov/lccn/sn86090474/1887-07-23/ed-1/seq-4/

Robinson, C. K. (1921, October 6). Mack Edwards Arrested in Clintwood, Virginia. (C. K. Robinson, Ed.) *Asheville Citizen-times*, p. 8.

State News. (1876, June 9). *Charlotte Observer, 8*(2249), p. 3.

State News. (1902, January 10). *Statesville Record And Landmark, 28*(46), p. 6.

State vs. J.C. Randolph (Mitchell County Superior Court November 16, 1907).

Tax Quarrel Was Fatal. (1907, June 30). *The Washington Post*(11343), p. 13.

The Linville River Railroad. (1897, January 25). *Messenger*(1), p. 1.

Top of Roan Mountain on the dividing line between North Carolina and Tennessee. (1905). Retrieved from https://www.loc.gov/item/2018651723/

Tragedy in Mitchell. (1907, July 4). *The Western Sentenel*, p. 3.

Tramp. (1886, July 14). A Tramp to Roan Mountain. *The Lenior topic, xi*(42), p. 1.

View from Cloudland Site. (2019, June 14).

Was It Only a Fake. (1893, January 6). *Marion Daily Star, 16*(40), p. 1.

Watson, H. (Ed.). (1921, August 7). Mountaineers Near Asheville Shoot, Kill and Wound. *The Index-Journal, 3*(173), p. 1.

Special Thanks For Verbal Information From:

Charlie Ledford (Deceased) - *Cloudland Information and Moonshining Stories*

Cleo Edwards (Deceased) and Edna Edwards (Deceased) - *Mack Edwards Story, Cloudland Hotel Information*

Clyde Edney (Deceased) - *Roan Mountain Whiskey Recipe and Details*

Janie Ledford Cook - *Compiling Research, Family History and Genealogy on all of the Stories in this Book*

Joe Garland - *Moonshine Still and Various Information*

Kenneth Ellis - *Susan Phillips Moonshine Story*

Ruby Burleson Ledford (Deceased) - *Anderson Burleson Information, Glen Ayre 1900s, Photos*

Roscoe Edwards (Deceased) - *Holland English Information, Mack Edwards Story, Roan Mountain Dew Information*

Tommy Lee Edwards (Deceased) - *Mack Edwards Story, Little Rock Creek Baptist Church Records*

Index

A

Arrowood, WA, 56
Ayers, Cleveland, 70
Ayers, Doc, 46
Ayers, J.C., 42, 43, 44, 71
Ayers, J.M., 44, 70, 76
Ayers, Marion, 71
Ayres, Guss, 56

B

Bailey, I.H., 70, 71
Bakersville, 30, 31, 34, 41, 44, 55, 58, 61, 64, 65, 68, 69, 83, 105, 106, 107, 109, 112, 113, 115, 117, 120, 121, 125, 126, 127, 128
Bartlett, Avery, 105
Bass, Julia, 107
Bethlehem Baptist Church, 46
Biddix, Gracie, 46
Biddix, John, 70
Biddix, Yates, 70
Black, William, 30
Blevins, Nat, 71
Boone, CC, 56
Bowman, Anna, 70
Bowman, J.C., 70
Bowman, J.L., 71
Bowman, Jake, 70
Bowman, Jakie, 56
Bowman, JD, 56
Bowman, Oscar, 70
Bowman, W.B., 70
Bowman, WG, 56
Bradshaw Jr, RH, 56

Burleson, Wylie Clingman, 55, 66
Burris. M, 56
Butler, CC, 56
Butt, Dr. VR, 56
Butt, V.R., 70
Butts, V.R., 71
Byrd, Hat, 115, 124
Byrd, L.C., 124
Byrd, N.W., 71
Byrd, RV, 56
Byrd, SB, 56

C

Campbell, WR, 56
Canipe, Henry, 70
Carrol, Bob, 114, 117
Carrol, Ellen, 109, 110, 114, 117, 125
Carroll, Bob, 126
Chaffin, WL, 56
Charles Creek, 36, 39, 44, 49, 95, 98, 100, 118
Childers, Aswell, 70
Childers, John, 46
Childers, Junior, 46
Claude McEntire Store, 44
Conley, JJ, 56
Conley, WW, 56
Cook, D.M., 44, 70
Cook, Janie Ledford, 93, 108
Cooke, David, 56
Cooke, Flem, 56
Cox, Elizabeth, 106
Cox, John, 56
Crawford, JW, 56

D

E

H

M

O

P

Q

R

T

W

Y

About the Author

Allen Cook lives in the *Shadow of the Roan*. Most of his leisure time is enjoyed with his wife, Danielle and daughter, Natalie. Living a rural lifestyle, Allen works for the local Community College in small business development, grows Christmas trees and writes about his heritage. His hobbies include exploring old home sites and mine digs around the Roan, hunting, fishing and occasionally picking guitar. Being grounded in a personal relationship with Jesus Christ, Allen's faith is his refuge and fortress in life.

Allen's first published book, *Moonshine, Murder & Mountaineers: The Wildest County in America* was released in 2014. Allen says that the biggest complement he received was that it was embraced by many locals and old timers. Allen is currently working on another book in the *Moonshine, Murder & Mountaineers* series. He can be contacted via email at wildestcounty@gmail.com or at www.facebook.com/wildestcountync.

Made in the USA
Middletown, DE
08 May 2023